Insurgent
MEXICO
1810~1815

San Miguel El Grande
Querétaro

Nautla

Gulf
of
Mexico

Acámbaro
Indaparapeo
Zitácuaro
Tiripitío
Tenancingo

San Cristóbal Ecatepec

Mexico City

Tlaxcala
Puebla

Veracruz

Córdoba

Orizaba

Cuernavaca
Cuautla
Mexcala R.

Huetamo
Taxco
Cutzamala
Ajuchitlán

Iguala

Tehuacán

Huajuapán

Tixtla
Chilapa

Chilpancingo

Yanhuitlán

Oaxaca

Acapulco

Ometepec

OCEAN

24,730

DATE DUE

Carl Hertzog

MORELOS OF MEXICO

Wilbert H. Timmons

*The coin in the front cover is a Mexican
peso which bears the portrait of Morelos.*

José M.ª
Morelos

J. CISNEROS

MORELOS

Priest Soldier Statesman
of
MEXICO

by

WILBERT H. TIMMONS

PROFESSOR OF HISTORY

Texas Western College

EL PASO : TEXAS WESTERN COLLEGE PRESS

1963

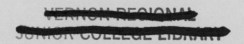

EDITED BY

SAMUEL D. MYRES

DRAWINGS BY

JOSE CISNEROS

*The insignia on the title page is the seal of the
Insurgent Congress which Morelos organized in 1813.*

PREFACE

M<small>Y</small> <small>INTEREST</small> *in José María Morelos, one of Mexico's most outstanding men, extends over much of the past fifteen years, a significant portion of which I have spent in research in the Latin American Collection of the University of Texas and the chief depositories of Mexico City and Morelia.*

This is the first full-length biography of Morelos in English, for which there has been a great need for some time. Although there are several biographies of Morelos by Mexican authors which have considerable merit, particularly the one by Alfonso Teja Zabre, language is frequently a barrier in the United States for those other than the specialist. The biographical sketches by James Magner and John Anthony Caruso are good, though quite brief. I have endeavored therefore to write a narrative which would be both scholarly and readable, in order to contribute to what is already known about Morelos and his career, and to provide a means whereby the college student and the general public in the United States might be able to gain a greater familiarity with this remarkable man.

No book could possibly be written and published without the assistance of many people, and to them I am extremely indebted. I wish to express my deep gratitude and sincere thanks to the following, who have been so helpful: Dr. Nettie Lee Benson, Librarian of the Latin American Collection of the University of Texas; Mrs. Dorothy Estes Knepper, Director of the San Jacinto Museum of History, San Jacinto Monument, Texas; Sr. Ignacio Rubio Mañé, Director, Archivo General de la Nación, and Sra. María Guzmán, Director, Archivo del Instituto de Antropología e Historia, both of Mexico City; Sr. Cristóbal Bermúdez Plata of the Archivo de Indias, Seville, Spain; and José Luis Magaña, Director of the Casa de Morelos in Morelia. I owe much to the late Professor Charles W. Hackett, who first suggested to

*me the need for a study of Morelos, and who supervised my
first manuscript on him.*

*To my colleagues on the faculty of Texas Western College
who assisted me with their advice, their skills, and their encouragement, I am deeply appreciative. President Joseph M. Ray
read the entire manuscript, made many valuable suggestions,
and arranged for the necessary financial assistance which made
publication possible. The Faculty Committee on Organized
Research made several grants of funds which greatly aided my
work, and a number of my colleagues in the Department of
History read portions of my manuscript and offered many
constructive criticisms. It was a rich and rewarding experience
for me to work with Carl Hertzog who designed this book.
I owe special thanks to Professor Samuel D. Myres, Chairman
of the Faculty Committee on Publications, for his editorial skill,
timely words of encouragement, and tireless efforts in preparing
the manuscript for the press.*

*Finally, I want to acknowledge and thank José Cisneros, who
drew the illustrations, Margarita Lopez, who typed the manuscript, and Shirley Gonzalez and Roberta Logerman, who
compiled the index. My wife Laura has been an invaluable aid
ever since I first became interested in the subject of this book,
and has never failed to be a source of inspiration, especially
when it was most needed.*

WILBERT H. TIMMONS

Texas Western College
El Paso, Texas
January, 1963

CONTENTS

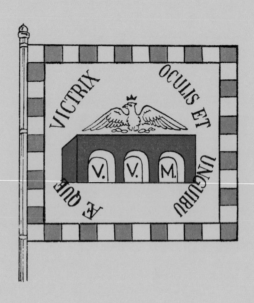

*Battle flag of Morelos, inscribed: "She conquers
equally with her eyes and her talons."*

INTRODUCTION

Eᴀʀʟʏ ɪɴ ᴛʜᴇ ɴɪɴᴇᴛᴇᴇɴᴛʜ ᴄᴇɴᴛᴜʀʏ *the village of San Agustín de las Cuevas, situated about fifteen miles south of Mexico City on the highway to Cuernavaca, was a quiet little place whose unhurried pace and leisurely existence were seldom disturbed. But on November 21, 1815, the scene was different. By late afternoon a large crowd had gathered in the square, including several hundred people from Mexico City, and there was an air of anticipation and excitement which the town had never known before. For everyone anxiously awaited the arrival of a famous insurgent — José María Morelos, the greatest leader of the movement for Mexican independence since Miguel Hidalgo.*

Presently, the sight of a large cloud of dust down the street and the noise of horses' hooves announced the approach of the renowned visitor, and in a few moments he came into view. He was mounted on horseback, but he did not ride at the head of an army, or smile at the populace, or wave to the señoritas. Instead, he was completely surrounded by an armed escort, which closely scrutinized every move he made. His legs were in shackles, and his face was drawn and without expression. Instead of cheers from the crowd, he received only vile and humiliating insults. For José María Morelos, chief of the revolution, was a prisoner of the viceroy, having been captured by royalist forces near Tesmalaca some two weeks before. Now he was being led to Mexico City to be tried for taking up arms against his government and his church.

The physical appearance of the prisoner was not greatly impressive. As he was helped off his horse and given a jug of water to quench his thirst, it could be seen that he was small in stature, heavy set, with rough facial features, thick lips, and deep brown coloring. He wore a handkerchief tied about his head, as he had done all during his revolutionary career. Most of the time he ignored what was taking place around him, and just stared into space. If he had a single thought, it was not concern for his own fate, for he knew what that would be, but for the future of the cause he had led.

But even if José María Morelos was not particularly imposing in looks, he was no ordinary man, as his captors were well aware; for the viceroy had rewarded them liberally with honors and titles for their efforts in taking him prisoner. Morelos had been a priest before he joined the revolution of Hidalgo in 1810. After the capture and death of Hidalgo in 1811 Morelos had emerged as the greatest military and political figure the independence period produced. He had organized and trained revolutionary armies and had won many great victories throughout southern Mexico. He had clarified the objectives of the revolution, sponsored a declaration of independence from Spain, formulated a comprehensive socio-economic program for the betterment of the Mexican people, and had established at Chilpancingo an insurgent Congress to enact his program into law. He had demonstrated exceptional talent as a leader and had won renown for his personal qualities of unselfish devotion and self-denial. Now in 1815 the Morelos revolution had been in decline for more than a year, and the greater part of its program had remained unfulfilled; but the cornerstone of an independent Mexican nation had been laid, and the flames of a Mexican national spirit had been kindled.

As the shadows lengthened over the main square of the village and announced the approach of evening, Morelos' armed escort completed preparations for the final leg of the journey to the capital. In accordance with viceregal instructions, Morelos was placed in a coach, and the remainder of the trip was undertaken at night to protect the prisoner from further humiliation from the jeering crowds.

The party at length arrived at the capital in the early morning hours of November 22, and Morelos was immediately confined in the secret prisons of the Inquisition under a heavy guard. Beginning on that same morning and continuing for more than a week, the accused man stood trial and gave testimony before three separate tribunals in answer to a relentless barrage of questions about his life and his revolutionary activities. Throughout the whole ordeal he maintained his characteristic calm and dignity, and with amazing accuracy in his recitation of details, he told the story of his life. As the testimony was given and recorded, the biography of a great man began to unfold. The story of this man, José María Morelos, is the subject of the chapters which follow, told largely in his own words and in those of his contemporaries.

CHAPTER I

THE EARLY YEARS

SITUATED some two hundred miles west of Mexico City is the city of Morelia, capital of the state of Michoacán, a region of superb scenic beauty. Morelia is not as familiar to the American tourist as Mexico City or Acapulco or points in between, but it is a lovely place which possesses much of the charm it has had since colonial times when it was known as Valladolid. This city was the birthplace of José María Morelos, one of Mexico's most remarkable national heroes, an outstanding military commander, leader of Mexican independence, and a celebrated political and social reformer.

It is recorded that in the city of Valladolid on October 4, 1765, Cura Francisco Gutiérrez de Robles baptized with oil and gave chrism to an infant who was born on September 30 and to whom was given the name José María Teclo, the legitimate son of Manuel Morelos and Juana Pavón, *españoles*.[1] Although the version given by the Mexican historian Carlos María Bustamante that Morelos was born on a ranch on the outskirts of Valladolid is still accepted by some authorities, most now agree that he was born within the city and was in fact a "native of Valladolid," as he stated on numerous occasions during his career.[2] The Morelian historian Licenciado Juan de la Torre, who obtained much of his information from Morelos' grand-nephew, Licenciado Francisco Pérez Morelos, indicates that Morelos' parents were residents of the hacienda of Sindurio near Valladolid, but moved to the city and lived in a small house next to the chapel of Prendimiento just before Morelos' birth. De la Torre writes that while walking along the street one day, Morelos' mother was suddenly overcome with labor pains and thereupon gave birth to an infant in the doorway of a nearby house.[3] Since 1881 this house, located on the southwest corner of García Obesa and La Corregidora

streets in Morelia, has been marked with a plaque which carries
an inscription stating that José María Morelos was born there
on September 30, 1765.

From ecclesiastical records it can be established that Morelos'
parents were respectable people, "of good reputation and Chris-
tians of long standing," though quite poor.[4] His father, Manuel
Morelos, was an "honest man," who worked as a carpenter in
Valladolid, a trade which he had probably learned from his
father, Guillermo Morelos. The general deportment of his family,
Morelos declared in 1815, "might not have been edifying, but
it was hardly scandalous."[5]

Considerably more information is available regarding Morelos' mother, Doña Juana María Pérez Pavón, from archival
materials which have come to light and have been published
recently.[6] Her ancestors for generations had been residents of
the town of San Juan Bautista de Apaseo in the jurisdiction of
the city of Celaya. She was the daughter of Juana María Molina
de Estrada and José Antonio Pavón. He at one time had been
connected with the Church, but apparently later became a
schoolmaster in Valladolid.[7] The future mother of Morelos lived
in an environment which permitted her to receive a better-than-
average education. Judging from her activities later in life, it
is evident that she was a remarkable woman, of strong character
and firm conviction, deeply devoted to her family and her son,
and unquestionably the greatest single influence on him in his
early years.[8] Subsequently, there were two more children, Nicolás and María Antonia Morelos.[9]

There has been considerable controversy about Morelos'
racial composition. Since Morelos said that his parents were
"Spanish by both lines," and since his baptismal certificate used
the word *españoles* to describe his parents, it might seem that
he was a creole — that is, a person of Spanish descent born in
America. But it is more likely that Morelos was a mestizo, of
mixed Spanish and Indian blood, and that the word *españoles*
as used by Morelos and in the baptismal certificate should be

interpreted in a political, rather than in a racial or ethnic sense —
meaning that his parents were Spanish subjects. Alfonso Teja
Zabre adds that the term *españoles* should not be taken seriously
because "of the custom during that period of concealing the true
ethnic background, since everyone desired to pass not only for
creoles but for European Spaniards as well."[10] Moreover, the
phrase *limpio de sangre*, used by Morelos when he was seeking
to be ordained, meant simply that he was devoid of Jewish or
Moorish blood. Only the pro-Spanish historian Lucas Alamán
contends that Morelos was of mixed Indian and negro blood,
even though he always called himself Spanish, since the leaders
of Mexican independence, though supporting the rights of the
Indians and crying out against the injustice of the Conquest,
"desired to derive their antecedents from the conquering nation
rather than the conquered people."[11] The most reasonable assumption regarding Morelos' ancestry is that it was "free of
mulatto and negro blood, or that of any other bad race," that
his mother was a creole, and that his father was part Indian.[12]

Most of Morelos' boyhood must have been spent helping his
father provide a livelihood for the family. No doubt there were
many hardships, and the problem of earning a sufficient family
income must have been acute much of the time. Yet there was
time in those early years for Morelos to acquire some elementary
instruction. From his mother he received some of the essentials
of an education, including how to read and write. On the death
of his father in 1779 the fourteen-year-old boy was entrusted to
the care of his uncle, Felipe Morelos, who lived on an hacienda
near Apatzingán.[13] This change of residence was José Morelos'
first introduction to the *tierra caliente* of southern Mexico.

Felipe Morelos apparently was a man of means, who owned
not only a hacienda but also a mule train which he employed
in the lucrative trade with the Orient, carrying the rich cargoes
of goods overland between Acapulco and Mexico City. The
young Morelos worked first as a *labrador* on the hacienda, and
later as an *arriero*, or mule driver.[14] At times he gained practical

experience in a most impulsive manner, according to a story General Nicolás Bravo later told Lucas Alamán. On one occasion when Morelos was chasing a bull, he struck his head on a low branch of a tree; the blow threw him from his horse, leaving him in a semi-conscious condition with a permanent scar across his nose.[15]

The overland route from Acapulco to Mexico City, known as the China Road, was one of the most important in the commercial life of colonial New Spain. It linked the capital with the celebrated port of Acapulco, the eastern terminus for the Manila galleons, which brought in the rich cargoes from the Orient. Stretching northward overland from Acapulco, the trail went up through the high and rugged Sierra Madre del Sur, through Chilpancingo, the *tierra caliente*, the Río de las Balsas, continuing up the great central plateau through Cuernavaca into the Valley of Mexico and the capital, a total distance of about three hundred miles. Undoubtedly, conditions of travel were primitive, accommodations few, and discomforts manifold. Yet this life as mule driver yielded a regular income, some of which young Morelos invested in mules, and some of which he sent to Valladolid for the support of his family.[16] It gave him a chance on occasion to study a little grammar; it toughened his body and conditioned him for a rigorous, outdoor existence; and it gave him a thorough knowledge of the *tierra caliente*, where some years later he was to lead his insurgent army against the forces of the viceroy. At length, in 1790, Morelos, a young man of twenty-five years, resolved to abandon the outdoor life in favor of the classroom, where he would begin studies for the priesthood and a career in the Church.

During the time Morelos was working as a *labrador* and *arriero*, his mother's fondest hope was that her son should become a priest. The major consideration in shaping his mother's desire was an inheritance in the form of a *capellanía*, or benefice, which Morelos' maternal great-grandfather had established and which was to be awarded to the descendants under certain pre-

THE ARRIERO

scribed conditions. These conditions were set forth in the will of Pedro Pérez Pavón, grandfather of Juana Pavón, Morelos' mother, dated March 2, 1750 in San Bautista de Apaseo:

It is my wish that a *capellanía de misas* be established from my property, which amounts to 4,000 pesos; the *capellanes* will be obligated to say forty masses annually in order to receive the income from this principal. . . . I name for the first *capellán* José Antonio Pérez, my natural son, twenty-four years of age, who is to be given title to it provided he is favorably disposed to an ecclesiastical career; should he not be so disposed, the right of this *capellanía* is to descend from the legitimate sons of my brothers, Sebastián and Francisco, and my sister, María Pérez Pavón, giving preference to the oldest rather than the youngest, the son of the male to that of the female, the nearest relationship rather than the most remote; and above all, . . . it is my wish that preference be given to that one who is nearest to being ordained. At this time I name as *patrón* the *juez eclesiástico* of the city of Celaya. . . . In case my lineage should become extinct, it is my wish that the *capellán* should be continually a creole child of this town, a Spanish subject, a legitimate son, and one favorably disposed to an ecclesiastical career. . . .[17]

In the succeeding years the value of the property was fixed at 2,800 pesos. On November 4, 1755, the *capellanía* was awarded to the person named in the will, José Antonio Pérez Pavón, although it is not known what his connection with the Church was, nor how long he continued to exercise the function of *capellán*. He did not remain single, however, but fathered at least one child, a daughter, who was Morelos' mother. In 1784 the inheritance passed to José Antonio Martínez Conejo, a descendant through the transverse line. But when his marriage in December, 1789, to Mariana de Caro created a vacancy, a struggle for possession of the inheritance developed among the descendants of the three different lines.[18] The chance of obtaining the award was the reason that Morelos' mother was so eager for him to undertake an ecclesiastical career. By fulfilling that particular condition in the will, Morelos could strengthen considerably his eligibility to the inheritance, which would provide him and his widowed mother a fixed income for the rest of their lives. It is hardly a coincidence, therefore, that soon after the vacancy developed, Morelos took leave of the *tierra caliente* and the life of the *arriero* to begin his instruction for a career in the Church.

In 1790 when Morelos was about twenty-five years of age he enrolled at San Nicolás College in Valladolid, an institution which had been founded two hundred and fifty years before by the illustrious Vasco de Quiroga.[19] Miguel Hidalgo, who later initiated the revolt that eventually led to Mexican independence, had been a teacher at the college for at least eleven years preceeding Morelos' arrival.[20] Appointed rector of the college in early 1790 Hidalgo served in that position for about two years, until he was ordered to the parish of Colima in 1792.[21] For a year and a half, therefore, the lives of these two great leaders of Mexican independence — Hidalgo, the rector, and Morelos, the student — overlapped at San Nicolás, although it would be a distortion to assume that a particularly close relationship developed between them at that time. No doubt Morelos was impressed by the considerable intellectual attainments and brilliance of his rector and held him in high esteem. On the other hand, since the college was small and Morelos' mature age was conspicuous, the student may have attracted the rector's eye; but there is nothing to suggest that the relationship was intimate, or that the liberal-minded Hidalgo deliberately indoctrinated Morelos or any of the other students with radical ideas. Nevertheless, Hidalgo's personality was such as to create an indelible impression on those with whom he came in contact, and it is not difficult to explain Morelos' great curiosity, some eighteen years later in 1810, about the revolutionary movement which swept through the province of Michoacán, once he had ascertained who its leader was.

At San Nicolás, Morelos studied grammar under Jacinto Mariano Moreno and Latin under José María Alzate.[22] Morelos must have worked hard at his studies and applied himself diligently, even if the following recommendation of his work written by his grammar teacher may have been a bit on the glowing side:

I certify that José María Morelos [it began] has passed under my direction the courses in the minimum and minor studies, and that he has conducted himself with such prudence and irreproachable conduct, that he has never done anything to deserve any kind of punishment; that he has performed the duties of a *decurión* with such application, that he has elevated himself above all the other students. In view of his progress and his interest in justice, it is a pleasure to recommend that he be rewarded with the highest honor in the classroom, . . . for he has performed his functions with the universal applause of all the participants.[23]

While Morelos was attending San Nicolás the issue involving the possession of the *capellanía* arose again as the result of a vacancy created by the marriage of the *capellán,* José Antonio Conejo, in December, 1789. In April, 1790, Juana Pavón advanced the candidacy of her son,[24] and two months later Morelos formally presented his case before the *juez de testamentos y capellanías,* Juan Antonio de Tapia, declaring that he was engaged in satisfying the requirement of advancing to the ecclesiastical state, to which he "had been inclined since his first years," and that he was an immediate descendant of the founder.[25] Nicolás Baquero, Morelos' attorney, presented testimony which attempted to show that his client's claim to the inheritance was better than that of either of his two rivals, Tiburcio Esquiros and José Joaquín Rodríguez Carnero. The argument stated that Morelos was the direct descendant of the founder and the grandson of the first *capellán,* while the rival candidates were descendants only through the transverse line. Moreover, it declared that since the first *capellán,* José Antonio Pérez Pavón, had been specifically named in the will, he could not be disqualified from the inheritance by virtue of his marriage to Juana María Molina de Estrada; and since he was illegitimate, he could contract marriage without impediment. Tiburcio Esquiros subsequently withdrew from the contest; but Luis Camargo, attorney for Rodríguez Carnero, presented testimony which challenged Morelos' claim. Camargo declared that his client was the great-grandnephew of the founder through a legitimate line, and that he was also the grandson of Doña María Pérez Pavón, whose descendants were expressly named as heirs to the property. On the other hand, he said that Morelos, being descended from the founder by an illegitimate succession because of the status of José Antonio Pérez Pavón, should be excluded. On October 18, 1791, the property was awarded to Rodríguez Carnero, who retained it until his death in 1804.[26] This outcome must have been a bitter disappointment not only for Morelos but also for his mother, who for the rest of her life never relaxed her efforts for a moment to obtain the *capellanía* for her son.

In October, 1792, Morelos left San Nicolás College to continue his studies at the Seminario Tridentino, also located in Valladolid. The reason for the change, according to one authority, was that Morelos was thus able to take an intermediate course in Latin, as well as certain other courses which were not being offered at San Nicolás at the time.[27] Morelos remained at the Seminario for about two and a half years, receiving instruction in rhetoric and philosophy. According to his teachers he applied himself with such diligence and industry that he led the class.[28]

In March, 1795, with the completion of three and a half years of work toward the Bachelor of Arts degree, Morelos proceeded to the Royal and Pontifical University of Mexico to take his final examinations, in accordance with a clause in the constitution of the university which allowed qualified students of certain provincial colleges with three years of instruction in the arts' courses to receive their degree at that institution.[29] On the basis of "examination, approval, and ability," Morelos was awarded the degree of Bachelor of Arts on April 28, 1795.[30]

The granting of ecclesiastical orders in New Spain during the 18th century followed the regulations established by the Council of Trent in the middle of the 16th century. They provided that a candidate for an ecclesiastical career could be eligible for the clerical tonsure at the age of fourteen, on condition that he had first received the sacrament of confirmation, could demonstrate ability to read and write, and could give testimony that he had received instruction in the rudiments of the faith.[31] The four minor orders — acolyte, exorcist, reader, and doorkeeper — were granted together in most cases, the prerequisites being a knowledge of Latin and a favorable recommendation from the candidate's priest or teacher. The major orders consisted of the subdeaconate, the deaconate, and the priesthood, the age requirement for these being twenty-two, twenty-three, and twenty-five years respectively. Ordinarily, an interval of one year was required between the last of the minor orders and the first of the major, and between each one of the major orders. A candidate for any one of the major orders was required to present testimony of his birth, age, character, and conduct, and to submit letters of recommendation attesting to his qualifications. When the candidate had satisfactorily fulfilled all requirements, his application for promotion was then approved by the bishop.[32]

Morelos, on November 6, 1795, submitted his request for the first ecclesiastical orders to the Bishop of Michoacán, stating his desire to be admitted to the first clerical tonsure, the four minor orders, and the subdeaconate, and enclosing prescribed credentials.[33] He apparently assumed that his age would allow an exception to be made in his case, inasmuch as a one-year interval was ordinarily required between the minor orders and the first of the major. The six letters of recommendation that accompanied his petition declared that the candidate was the "legitimate son of Manuel Morelos and Juana Pavón, that he was of pure blood by both lines, that he had been educated in the teachings of the Church Fathers, that he was stable in deportment, modest in his actions, God-fearing, and that he took the sacraments frequently."[34]

To determine the character of an ecclesiastical candidate, church regulations required that his name be published on three

successive religious holidays in each place where the candidate
had resided; and should anything detrimental or unfavorable
to his name be shown within twenty-four hours after the third
religious day, the applicant would automatically become inel-
igible for promotion. Furthermore, any person who disapproved
a candidate but failed to voice his objections became liable to
the penalty of excommunication.[35] Morelos' name was submitted
in Valladolid and Apatzingán on three religious holidays in
November, 1795, and no adverse comments about him were
registered in either place.[36] He therefore received the first
clerical tonsure and the four minor orders on December 13 in the
episcopal palace of the Bishop of Michoacán, and on December
19 he received the subdeaconate.[37]

A short time later Morelos accepted an offer from Nicolás
Santiago de Herrera, *cura* of the town of Uruapan, to teach
grammar and rhetoric to the children there, an appointment
which the bishop confirmed on April 6, 1796, with the granting
of a license to teach.[38] The salary was probably not much, but
for the first time since he began his training for the priesthood
Morelos was able to send something home to his widowed
mother and maiden sister. Evidently he performed his duties
satisfactorily during his two years at Uruapan, for Cura Herrera
wrote that he had been found worthy of the title of Professor
of Grammar and Rhetoric, that he had made his points well,
held consultations with the students, preached the gospel force-
fully, set a good example for all, and assisted with the sacred
rites in an proficient manner.[39] On September 21, 1796, Morelos
was elevated to the deaconate, a special dispensation again
having been granted by the bishop, since Morelos' length of service in the subdeaconate had amounted to only nine months.[40]
Then, with the completion of the one-year requirement in the
deaconate, Morelos, in August, 1797, submitted his request for
his appointment to the priesthood.[41]

At this time it seemed opportune for Morelos' mother to renew
her fight to obtain for her son the inheritance which, it will be

remembered, had been established by her grandfather. Another three-cornered struggle resulted. It involved, in addition to Morelos, the current *capellán*, José Joaquín Rodríguez Carnero, who had held the property since 1791, and José Ignacio Conejo, son of a former *capellán*. Morelos' mother presented the following case in behalf of her son:

It has been stated and ascertained that the naming of sons and descendants of the brothers of the founder does not exclude the descendants through the direct line. . . . This should take preference over the transverse line regardless of the presence of illegitimacy. . . .

Moreover, the pious founder desired to reward that one of his relatives who was closest to being ordained. . . . This stipulation, emphasized so strongly by the founder, has been met by Bachiller Morelos y Pavón, who by reason of his qualifications was granted at the scheduled time the sacred order of the deaconate, and soon he will receive the priesthood. . . .

None of these circumstances are true of the rival claimants, Rodríguez and Conejo. The first one, not more than twenty-one years of age, has not as yet completed his grammar course, while the second, who is only six years of age, is scarcely old enough to go to school.

In addition, these claimants are descended by the transverse line, and are four generations removed from the founder; therefore my son, who is descended through the direct line, should take preference over them. . . .[42]

In spite of Juana Pavón's convincing arguments, the authorities rejected her petition, and the coveted property remained in the hands of Rodríguez Carnero until his death in 1804, when another struggle for possession was precipitated. It would be interesting to know if the racial factor was an obstacle blocking Morelos in his efforts to secure the inheritance.

Meanwhile, on December 20, 1797, the Bishop of Michoacán approved Morelos' request for the priesthood, declaring that the candidate's aptitude and fitness had been determined by examination, and that he had taken the spiritual exercises and fulfilled all conditions set forth by the Council of Trent.[43] Morelos was accordingly appointed to the priesthood on the following day and shortly afterward was granted licenses to celebrate mass, hear confession, and preach in Uruapan and neighboring curacies.[44]

Morelos did not remain in Uruapan long. On January 31, 1798, he was assigned as *cura interino* to the parish of Tamácuaro de la Aguacana in the district of Churumuco.[45] Located in the heart of the *tierra caliente*, the assignment has been described as in "the hottest and perhaps the most miserable of all Michoacán pueblos,"[46] but Morelos wrote that he accepted the position with rejoicing, and promised to devote his life to the "cultivation of the vineyard of the Lord and in obedience to His Illustrious Majesty, who had so graciously chosen humble persons for great undertakings."[47] Shortly afterward, Morelos, accompanied by his mother and sister, set out for the new assignment.

The contrast between the Pátzcuaro-Uruapan region and the *tierra caliente* to the south almost defies description. The traveler leaves one world and enters another as he descends from the cool, green, scenic, mountainous area around Pátzcuaro southward to Tacámbaro, into a hot, barren, unproductive region which still repels civilization. It is significant that even today there are no roads south of Tacámbaro worthy of the name, and that travel is possible only by jeep or mule-back. The Indians of the area live as they have for centuries, eke out an existence somehow, receiving from the Río de las Balsas, which flows through the area, some small relief from the heat, the dirt, and the bad odors.

For almost a year Morelos remained at Churumuco in faithful and conscientious performance of his duties. His mother, however, fell ill from the intense heat, and when her condition failed to improve, Morelos sent her and his sister back to Valladolid. In time, he received news that his family had reached Pátzcuaro, but that his mother was so near death that a member of the family had already gone to look for wax to be used for her last rites.[48] Shortly afterward, on January 5, 1799, Juana Pavón died in Pátzcuaro, and was buried in that town.[49] She was by far the greatest single influence on Morelos during the first thirty-five years of his life.

Just before his mother's death Morelos wrote the bishop requesting that he be assigned to a parish in a cooler climate, inasmuch as he had heard that Cura Eugenio Reyes Arroyo had been appointed to the parish of Churumuco, and the heat of the *tierra caliente* had caused his mother to become so seriously ill that she was not expected to recover.[50] Word was received from the bishop, perhaps in March, 1799, ordering an exchange of curacies by which Reyes Arroyo was assigned to Churumuco, and Morelos was appointed *cura* and *juez eclesiástico* of the parish of Carácuaro, some thirty miles to the east. His request for a cooler climate had either been ignored or rejected; but in dutiful compliance with orders, Morelos shortly afterward departed for his new assignment.

REFERENCES

1. Birth certificate of José María Morelos y Pavón, Valladolid, October 4, 1765, in Lucas Alamán, *Historia de Mexico*, IV, appendices, pp. 47-48. A facsimile of the document is given in J. M. Coéllar (ed.), *Autógrafos de Morelos*.
2. Carlos María Bustamante, *Cuadro histórico de la revolución Mexicana*, III, 244; Testimony of Morelos, Luis Castillo Ledón (compiler), *Morelos documentos inéditos y poco conocidos*, III, 11. The Testimony of Morelos consists of the statements which he made before the civil and ecclesiastical authorities at his trial in 1815. This narrative, recorded by a secretary in the third person, contains numerous inaccuracies, but it is an invaluable source for Morelos' life. Hereafter it will be cited as *Morelos documentos*.
3. Juan de la Torre, *Bosquejo histórico y estadístico de la ciudad de Morelia*, p. 218.
4. Testimony of Lorenzo Sendejas, Valladolid, November 6, 1795, *Morelos documentos*, I, 5.
5. Testimony of Morelos, *ibid.*, III, 31.
6. Last will and testament of Pedro Pérez Pavón, San Juan Bautista de Apaseo, March 2, 1750, in Martín Luis Guzmán (ed.), *Morelos y la iglesia Católica—Documentos*, pp. 161-64.
7. Testimony of Morelos, *Morelos documentos*, III, 31.
8. See the letters written by her in her son's behalf in Guzmán (ed.), *Morelos y la iglesia Católica*, pp. 196-201.
9. Testimony of Morelos, *Morelos documentos*, III, 11.
10. Alfonso Teja Zabre, *Vida de Morelos*, p. 13.
11. Alamán, *Historia de Mexico*, II, 316.
12. Petition of Don Nicolás Baquero, Valladolid, September 10, 1790, Guzmán (ed.), *Morelos y la iglesia Católica*, p. 175.
13. Alamán, *Historia de Mexico*, IV, 336.
14. Bustamante, *Cuadro histórico*, III, 244.
15. Alamán, *Historia de Mexico*, II, 316.
16. Bustamante, *Cuadro histórico*, III, 244.
17. Last will and testament of Pedro Pérez Pavón, San Juan Bautista de Apaseo, March 2, 1750, Guzmán (ed.), *Morelos y la iglesia Católica*, pp. 161-64.

18. See legal proceedings given in *ibid.*, pp. 165-71.
19. Testimony of Morelos, *Morelos documentos*, III, 11-12; Julián Bonavit, *Fragmentos de la historia del Colegio Primitivo y Nacional de San Nicolás de Hidalgo*, pp. 48-49.
20. See Miguel Hidalgo document, Valladolid, August 28, 1779, in *ibid.*, p. 246.
21. Nicolás Rangel (ed.), "Miguel Hidalgo y Costilla, 1753-1811," *Boletín del Archivo General de la Nación*, I (1930), 29.
22. Testimony of Morelos, *Morelos documentos*, III, 15; Bonavit, *Fragmentos*, 48.
23. Statement of Bachiller Jacinto Mariano Moreno, Valladolid, August 24, 1791, Guzmán (ed.), *Morelos y la iglesia Católica*, p. 189.
24. Petition of Juana María Pérez Pavón, Valladolid, April 17, 1790, *ibid.*, p. 168.
25. Petition of José María Morelos y Pavón, Valladolid, July 13, 1790, *ibid.*, pp. 169-70.
26. Opinion of Dr. Gabriel Gomez de la Puente, Valladolid, October 18, 1791, *ibid.*, pp. 185-87.
27. Bonavit, *Fragmentos*, pp. 48-50.
28. Statement of Licenciado José María Pisa, Valladolid, November 5, 1795, *Morelos documentos*, I, 9-10.
29. *Estatutos y Constituciones Reales de la Imperial y Regia Universidad de Mexico*, Art. CCXLI, 44.
30. A facsimile of Morelos' Bachelor of Arts degree is given in Nicolás Rangel, *José María Morelos*, p. 10. It may be noted that the only time in Morelos' life that he was in Mexico City was when he received this degree, with the exception of the latter months of 1815 when he was a prisoner of the royalists.
31. *El Sacrosanto y Ecumenico Concilio de Trento*, translated from the Latin by Ignacio López de Ayala, pp. 275-76.
32. *Ibid.*, pp. 276-83, *passim*.
33. Petition of Bachiller José María Morelos, Valladolid, November 6, 1795, *Morelos documentos*, I, 3; a facsimile of the document is in J. M. Coéllar (ed.), *Autógrafos de Morelos*.
34. See testimonies given in *Morelos documentos*, I, 4-9.
35. *Ibid.*
36. *Ibid.*, pp. 9-10.
37. *Ibid.*, pp. 12-14. It is to be noted that an exception was made in Morelos' case to the rule that there must be an interval of one year between the last of the minor orders and the first of the major.
38. Statement of Bachiller Nicolás Santiago de Herrera, Uruapan, August 10, 1797, *ibid.*, pp. 20-21.
39. *Ibid.*
40. Santiago Camiña, Secretary, by order of Bishop Antonio de San Miguel, Valladolid, September 21, 1796, *ibid.*, p. 19.
41. Petition of José María Morelos, Uruapan, August, 1797, *ibid.*, pp. 19-20.
42. Petition of Juana María Pérez Pavón, Valladolid, September 11, 1797, Guzmán (ed.), *Morelos y la iglesia Católica*, pp. 199-201.
43. Santiago Camiña, Secretary, by order of Bishop San Miguel, Valladolid, December 21, 1797, *Morelos documentos*, I, 22-23.
44. See Enrique Arreguín (ed.), *A Morelos — Importantes revelaciones históricas*, pp. 80-82.
45. Morelos to Bishop Antonio de San Miguel, Uruapan, February 1, 1798, *Morelos documentos*, II, 249.
46. Dan Stanislawski, *The Anatomy of Eleven Towns in Michoacán*, p. 21.
47. Morelos to Bishop Antonio de San Miguel, Uruapan, February 1, 1798, *Morelos documentos*, II, 249.
48. Antonio Conejo to Morelos, Pátzcuaro, December, 1798, *ibid.*, p. 250, note 1.
49. Death certificate of Juana Pavón, Pátzcuaro, January 5, 1799, *ibid.*, note 2.
50. Morelos to Santiago Camiña, Tamácuaro de la Huacana, January 3, 1799, *ibid.*, pp. 249-50.

CHAPTER II

THE CURA OF CARACUARO

THE APOSTOLIC Roman Catholic Church was the most important and powerful institution in colonial New Spain. Its elaborate administrative hierarchy and organization, its doctrine and dogma, and its sacramental system, as developed by medieval European civilization, were transplanted by Spanish ecclesiastics who accompanied and followed the conquistadors to the New World and were firmly established. Dedicated clergy, regular and secular, came in the wake of Hernando Cortez, broke down frontiers, built churches and missions, and spread the faith with great zeal. As a moral and spiritual force, as an institution of property and wealth, and as a guardian of orthodoxy, political and religious, the Catholic church exercised a dominion over the hearts, minds, and lives of Spain's New World subjects that remained unchallenged and unequalled in colonial times.

Social inequalities existed within church organization, as indeed they did within colonial society generally. The upper clergy, which included for the most part the archbishops and bishops, were born in Spain of aristocratic and influential families. They received the most lucrative positions, the highest salaries, the greatest number of favors and privileges, and they lived in sumptuousness as did their counterparts in Europe. The historian H. H. Bancroft contends that in 1808 all the bishoprics of New Spain with one exception, the greater portion of the canon stalls, and a large number of the rich curacies were in the hands of Spaniards from Europe.[1] On the other hand, the lower clergy in most cases were creoles or mestizos, socially distinct and inferior to the Spanish-born prelates. Lacking the training and education of the Europeans, they usually found the opportunities for favors and preferment limited, and therefore received the less lucrative assignments. The renowned traveler and scientist Baron Alexander von Humboldt was extremely distressed to find in Mexico that the annual revenue from a diocese of an archbishop might amount to as much as 130,000 pesos, while there were priests in Indian villages whose income scarcely came to 100 or 120 pesos a year.[2]

The Bishopric of Michoacán was one of the largest, wealthiest, and most important in New Spain. At the end of the 18th century it contained about 120 curacies, practically all of them administered by the secular branch of the clergy. There were more than 1,000 priests in the bishopric to take care of the spiritual needs of some 400,000 parishioners, of whom about half were Indians.[3] The resulting ratio of one priest for every 400 parishioners seemingly would have been satisfactory had it not been for the uneven distribution throughout the diocese. One authority has indicated that there were always 500 ecclesiastics in Michoacán who were without occupation,[4] most of whom probably were trying to avoid assignment to a post outside the capital. At the same time a shortage of priests almost always existed in the less desirable, more remote, and poorer parishes, with the result that individual priests in the outlying areas frequently had to perform functions and duties ordinarily assigned to several individuals. In all probability, a ratio of one priest for 2,000 or more parishioners was not uncommon.

The *cura,* or village priest, was one of the unsung heroes of colonial times. Humble in his origins, creole or mestizo by birth, and lacking the background, position, and education of his Spanish-born confreres, the *cura* was a conscientious, dedicated soul who had little to look forward to except burdensome duties, meager wages, and uncertain opportunities for advancement. True, a position in the Church was eagerly sought by the more aspiring and ambitious among the lower classes, but the education necessary for the priesthood more often than not involved great financial hardship, and the reward was likely to be a poor, impoverished parish, whose Indian population was backward, ignorant, and poverty stricken, if not lazy. Obviously, the parish priest in such an environment was the most important person in the community — pastor, doctor, mayor, judge, and jack-of-all trades, all wrapped up into one. His was burdensome, demanding, exhausting work. No one in a position of authority in colonial New Spain knew or understood individual human strengths and weaknesses quite so well as the village *cura;* no one was in closer touch with the people or more intimately acquainted with their problems, their joys, and their sorrows. No wonder that so many of the revolutionary leaders of a later day were those who earlier in their careers had seen service as parish priests!

The Bishop of Michoacán at the end of the 18th century was Antonio de San Miguel, one of the most able and enlightened persons in the history of that office. He had a reputation for benevolence, an interest in the public welfare, and a genuine understanding of basic social and economic problems which was rare among those who held high office in those days. His *Informe* written in 1799 to the king of Spain, which Alexander von Humboldt incorporated into his *Ensayo político sobre el reino de la Nueva España,* is a classic description of social conditions by a keen and understanding observer, and it merits reproduction here:

The population of New Spain is composed of three classes of people — white or Spanish, Indians, and the castes, or mixed. The Spaniards comprise one-tenth of the total number, and nearly all the property and wealth is in their hands. The Indians and the castes cultivate the land, serve the wealthy, and live by manual labor. Because of this a conflict of interests results — a mutual hatred which is developing rapidly between those who have everything and those who have nothing. . . . There is no middle class; one is either rich or miserable, noble or infamous.

The benefits which the laws seek to give the Indians are extremely limited, and it can almost be said that they do more harm than good. . . . The natives do not have individual property, and they are obliged to cultivate the holdings of the community. This method of cultivation comes to be an even more unbearable task for them because for many years in this area they have almost lost hope of receiving any profit from their labor. . . .

The law prohibits intermarriage between castes; it prohibits the whites from living in the Indian towns; and it prohibits the Indians from living among the Spaniards. Civilization is opposed to this barrier which has been placed between them. . . .

The castes are marked as inferior by law, and they are subjected to the tribute, which places on them an indelible blot. Among the mixed races there are many families which by color and stature could be confused with the Spaniards, but the law scorns them. Although many of them are gifted and are people of good character, they are forced to live in a state of constant irritation against the whites; it is a wonder that their resentment does not move them to vengeance more often.

In the past the *alcaldes mayores* considered themselves to be the only officials with the exclusive privilege of buying and selling in their districts. These usurious officials forced the Indians to buy at arbitrary prices a certain number of beasts of burden, with the result that all the natives fell into debt. On the pretext of making them pay, the *alcaldes mayores* forced the Indians into slavery. With the establishment of the *intendencies,* the *alcaldes* were replaced by the subdelegates, who were forbidden to participate in any sort of commercial activity. But since no salary was paid them the change made the situation worse. The *alcaldes* administered justice with impartiality provided that it did not interfere with their own interests; but the subdelegates, not having any income other than what they can get through graft, believe that they are authorized to use illicit means to provide for themselves. Only on rare occasions can the Indians expect protection and help from the subdelegates. The Indians therefore look to the *curas* for help, with the result that the clergy and the subdelegates live in continuous opposition to one another.

Let it not be said that the fear of punishment is sufficient to preserve peace in these areas — other expedients are necessary. If the new legislation that Spain impatiently awaits does not deal with the condition of the Indians and the people of color, the power of the clergy will not be enough to keep them in submission and respectful of authority, though great is the affection for the church in the hearts of these unhappy people.

The bishop then set forth his recommendations for improving the existing social and economic problems:

Let the hated duty — the personal tribute — be abolished; let the infamous law which brands the people of color be abolished so they may occupy all the civil posts which do not require a special title of nobility; let the communal holdings be distributed among the natives; let a portion of the royal lands be given to the Indians and castes; let there be adopted for Mexico an agrarian law . . . whereby a poor laborer can break up the lands which the large proprietors hold, and which have been uncultivated for centuries to the detriment of the national economy; let the Indians, castes, and whites be given full freedom to live in the towns, which now belong exclusively to only one of these classes; let fixed salaries be provided for all judges and magistrates of a district. I have submitted here the major points on which the happiness of the Mexican people depends.[5]

But the remedial legislation which the bishop sought never came, nor did it come with the establishment of Mexican independence. Solving the problems which the Mexican nation inherited from its colonial past became its great task in the nineteenth and twentieth centuries; and it was rare when action was taken by means other than violence and revolution.

The parish of Carácuaro, where Morelos lived and worked as *cura* and *juez eclesiástico* for eleven years beginning in early 1799, was located about thirty miles east of Churumuco near the Río de las Balsas on one of its main tributaries. Founded in 1735,[6] its location was not appreciably more healthful than that of Churumuco, and it was just as poor, and more heavily populated. A *padrón general* of the Carácuaro parish, drawn up by Eugenio Reyes Arroyo in August, 1798, a few months before the parish was assigned to Morelos, indicates that it had more than 1,800 parishioners,[7] most of whom lived in one of three towns clustered together near a tributary of the river. Nocupétaro lay about a league to the north of Carácuaro, the two being separated by a river, while Acuyo lay about six leagues to the southeast of Carácuaro.[8] The remaining parishioners were residents of one of several ranches and haciendas that lay in varying distances from the towns. To administer sacraments, instruct in doctrine, hear confessions, baptize the infants, marry the young couples, bury the dead, and take care of all the personal needs of so many people spread over such a wide area was almost an impossible task, all combining to explain why Morelos on more than one occasion sent requests for an assistant, and suggested that the size of the jurisdiction be reduced.[9]

The people of the parish supported their priest in a rather distinctive way. Morelos' subsistence for five months of the year was provided by the parishioners of Carácuaro, for five months by those of Nocupétaro, and for the remaining two months by those of Acuyo, since it was smallest and poorest. His monthly salary of twenty-four pesos and three reales was paid by the people through the collection of a special tax called the *tasación* for the support of church officials. In addition, Morelos was provided with a few personal services, such as the use of kitchen utensils, and the help of a messenger boy, a stable boy, and a woman for grinding the corn.[10]

Morelos had served in his new assignment only a short time when several of the leading officials of Carácuaro drafted a protest against him. In a letter addressed to the Bishop of Michoacán, the *gobernador* of Carácuaro, the *alcalde,* and others, including several former *gobernadores,* complained of the widespread misery and poverty of the parish, caused not only by natural and climatic forces such as the recent plague, the scarcity of water, the loss of harvests and the resulting high mortality, but also by the severity of the priest and the burdensome taxes which the parishioners had to pay for his support. "He scolds us; he annoys us; and he even mistreats us," they complained. Could he not be maintained, they argued, from the proceeds of the *arancel,* the regular fee assessed by the Church for marriage, confirmation, and burial rites, so that the hated *tasación* could be removed entirely?[11]

The bishop's office acknowledged receipt of the protest and instructed Morelos to explain. On November 22, 1799, Morelos

THE PRIEST

answered the charges point by point. To begin with, he accused the natives of disobedience, laziness, and insolence, pointing out that their obligation to him for the personal services had not been performed for the past twenty days. Moreover, their description of the mortality, the water scarcity, and the loss of crops were grossly exaggerated, since the poverty, misery, and suffering were largely caused by their lack of effort and willingness to work. All of his salary, he said, was used to buy ecclesiastical necessities such as hoods, oils, trays, and fat for candles, and a small part was spent for food. He insisted that he could not maintain himself solely from what the *arancel* might produce, but he agreed to reduce his own income by one-fourth to ease the tax burden of the people. If the bishop desired additional details, he could write Eugenio Reyes Arroyo, who had been the *cura* of Carácuaro for a number of years and who therefore knew the situation well.[12]

Cura Reyes Arroyo in his report to the bishop upheld Morelos on every point. He said that the Indians of the parish could maintain themselves and their families very easily on profits from the production of salt and a dye known as *cascolote,* but they refused to work, and stayed drunk most of the time. Moreover, all the salary of the *cura* was consumed in maintaining his personal servants and their husbands and wives, who also ate at the parish house. To remove the *tasación* would be a serious mistake and would only make the parishioners more arrogant and disrespectful than before. Only God would ever know, said Reyes Arroyo, how much trouble they caused him while he was their *cura.* Morelos' reply to their complaints was complete and fair, he concluded; but if Morelos desired to relax the rules, it should be only for such time as he held that office. Otherwise, relaxing the rules would be injurious to anyone who might hold that position in the future. When the bishop's office received Reyes Arroyo's defense, it dropped the case entirely.[13]

Another problem that came to Morelos' attention shortly after he took over his duties pertained to the hacienda of Cutzián

with its five hundred residents living within Morelos' ecclesiastical jurisdiction but at a distance of some ten leagues, a full
day's journey from Carácuaro. When the owner of the hacienda
complained to the bishop about the lack of spiritual care, Morelos was called upon to explain. He replied that a dangerous
river made travel to the hacienda difficult in good weather,
and that during the rainy season the road was practically im-
passable. For that reason the first *cura* of Carácuaro, Bachiller
Francisco Xavier de Ochoa, left a sum of 8,000 pesos for the
construction and maintenance of a chapel there and the support
of a chaplain. But the residents of the hacienda had allowed the
chapel to fall into disrepair, and the license for a chaplain to
celebrate mass and bury the dead had been lost for some time.
As a result, the residents of the hacienda had for years been
deprived of instruction in Christian doctrine and had been living
and dying without the sacraments. Some of the infants had been
baptized from time to time by a priest from another jurisdiction,
Morelos said, but he warned that if this practice were allowed
to continue, serious complications and confusion in ecclesiastical
administration would result. Whether Morelos' recommendation for the granting of a new license and appointment of a
chaplain to take care of the spiritual needs of the hacienda of
Cutzián was approved by the bishop is not clear.[14] In all probability, Morelos himself had to assume the responsibility for
the souls of Cutzián.

Some years later, in 1807, Morelos suggested that the two
haciendas of Cutzián and Santa Cruz be removed from his
jurisdiction and placed within the curacy of Turicato, and that
the two ranches of Atijo and Parota, which were a part of the
hacienda of Santa Cruz, be put under the jurisdiction of the
parish of Churumuco. These changes were necessary, he pointed
out, first, because the two haciendas were much closer to the
parishes he recommended than they were to Carácuaro; second-
ly, because during the rainy season three rivers which had to
be crossed became so swollen and flooded that travel became

extremely hazardous; and thirdly, because most of the faithful living on the haciendas went to confession and had their children baptized in places like Tacámbaro, Turicato, and Valladolid where they traded. "I can affirm," wrote Morelos, "that I am motivated by no consideration other than what my conscience dictates, because my experience of eight years here has led me to conclude that these haciendas within this curacy can not be administered effectively in view of the conditions I have mentioned. Although provision was made twenty years ago for a chaplain for the hacienda of Cutzián supported by means of an endowment of 8,000 pesos, those souls there have suffered all these years because the *curas* have not been able to carry out the provision, nor have they seen the end of the requests which seek to put this into effect."[15]

Morelos' request was submitted to the *promotor fiscal* in Valladolid for his opinion and recommendation. He admitted that there was much justification in the request, but pointed out that the division of the jurisdiction would leave Morelos and his successors without an endowment and would therefore cause irreparable damage to the entire parish; and if the minister should be appointed as the *cura* recommended, there would not be sufficient funds to cover parochial necessities. As a matter of fact, said the *promotor fiscal,* only 3,576 pesos in principal was established in the beginning, and expenses had been so heavy that only 344 pesos remained. Therefore, it was essential that the Carácuaro jurisdiction remain undivided, so that whatever surpluses it produced could be turned over to the *juez de capellanías* to fulfill the pious objectives in greater conformity to the wishes of the original testator.[16] The bishop's office subsequently informed Morelos that his request had been rejected, and that his superiors had ruled against any partition of his jurisdiction such as he had suggested.[17]

In 1802 Morelos built a church in Nocupétaro, which he described as measuring 120 varas from east to west and 110 varas from north to south, and which was the best church in the *tierra caliente*, with the exception of the one at Cutzamala. After the completion of the church, work was started on the cemetery, which was so solidly constructed, he reported, that there was none other like it in the *tierra caliente*, and only very few could match it in the colder regions. To the east of the cemetery were located the houses of the bellman and the grave digger; to the west, near the cemetery was the parish house; to the south at one corner was the old church building, where the cadavers could be placed pending burial; at the other corner was the new church; and nearby was the house of the sacristan. Most of the expenses of construction for these buildings had come out of Morelos' own pocket, and had left him heavily in debt, he said, so that it would be difficult for him to make any changes or additions, should the bishop's office disapprove of what had been done thus far.[18]

After the completion of the church Morelos submitted a request for the transfer of the parish capital from Carácuaro to Nocupétaro, pointing out numerous advantages such a change would bring. The climate was less severe at Nocupétaro; it was closer to the geographical center of the parish; there were more facilities in addition to the new church; and the town had a greater number of people — seventy families in all. Morelos then complied with instructions to secure the approval of the territorial judge and the principal officials of the area for the suggested transfer, and all appropriate documents were forwarded to the office of the bishop. The bishop's attorney replied that the request was just and had considerable merit, but that authorization for the change would have to come from the king, the viceroy, or the president of the *audiencia*, in accordance with Law 13, Title 3, Book G of the *Recopilación de las Indias*.[19] The bishop's office recommended approval of the transfer in a letter to the viceroy, but whether that approval was ever granted is not known, since Morelos' correspondence written from 1803 to 1810 was sent from Carácuaro at one time and from Nocupétaro at another. Perhaps Morelos' patience with Spanish colonial administration, both civil and ecclesiastical, was beginning to wear a little thin.

With regard to Morelos' personal affairs while he was a priest at Carácuaro, the Morelian historian Licenciado Juan de la Torre has written that Morelos, on August 17, 1801, purchased a house in Valladolid from a certain Juan José Martínez for 1,830 pesos, though the historian does not indicate where the money came from nor what use Morelos made of the place in the subsequent years.[20] It is probable that after 1807 Morelos rented the house to his sister, María Antonia, who in that year married Miguel Cervantes, a native of Guanajuato. The house had but one story when Morelos bought it, but in periodic trips to Valladolid he added a second story which he completed in 1809.[21] Properties in Valladolid inherited from his mother, Juana Pavón, were ceded by Morelos and his brother Nicolás to their sister and her husband in a document signed in Nocupétaro, June 20, 1808,[22] so that at the time of Morelos' trial in 1815, the house was the only property he owned.[23] It suffered heavy damage during the movement for independence and was confiscated by royalist forces. Placed up for sale at public auction in 1821, it was bought and restored by Morelos' sister and her husband and handed down to their daughter. Today, it is the celebrated "Casa de Morelos," located at the corner of Morelos Sur and Licenciado Soto Saldaña, and is now a national museum where the visitor may view a number of interesting personal effects which belonged to Morelos.

As a result of amorous relations between Morelos and an Indian woman of his parish named Brígida Almonte, there was born on May 15, 1803, the first of several children Morelos recognized at his trial in 1815. In accordance with the established practice of naming illegitimate children after the surname of the mother, this infant was named, and became known to history as, Juan Nepomuceno Almonte. A second child, a daughter, was born in 1809 in Carácuaro of an unknown mother, and was living in Nocupétaro in 1815, according to Morelos' testimony.

A third child was born during the revolutionary period in Oaxaca in 1814, as a result of Morelos' relations with a woman named Francisca Ortiz.[24] Moreover, Alfonso Teja Zabre has brought evidence to light which seems to indicate there may have been a fourth child, known as José Victoriano Flores, born in Nocupétaro on September 5, 1808, as a result of Morelos' relations with a woman named María Ramona Galván. Teja Zabre is not entirely convinced of the evidence, however, and warns that in the period after the establishment of independence, it became quite customary for people to submit claims of relationship with national heroes for the purpose of obtaining pensions and hereditary privileges.[25] The indiscretions of Morelos, of course, represent flagrant violations of priestly vows, and leave much to be desired in the matter of personal conduct. Yet his case was not an isolated one, and his habits were no worse than those of a considerable number of parish priests of his day. The Church, while uncompromising on matters of doctrine, took a lenient position on the weaknesses of man; and moral laxity among the Spanish clergy was not uncommon in colonial times.

With the death of José Joaquín Rodríguez Carnero in 1804, the *capellanía* which Morelos had been seeking, again became vacant. For a short time, possession of the property was contested between Morelos and José Romualdo Carnero, brother of the deceased *capellán;* but in August, 1805, Morelos, deciding that his rival had the better claim, withdrew, leaving the property to Carnero. The next year, however, the new *capellán* forsook his bachelor status and contracted marriage, thus creating a vacancy once more; so Morelos pressed his claim again. This time there were no rival contestants, and on April 9, 1806, Licenciado Miguel Mendez awarded Morelos the inheritance for which he had been struggling for sixteen years. On September 19, 1809, in Valladolid Morelos took formal possession of the *capellanía,* by that time reduced to 2,764 pesos of principal from the original amount of 4,000 pesos. Some two weeks later, after a bewildering number of deductions for fees, pensions, alms, and expenses for repairing the *capellán's* house, Morelos received as liquid capital the exact sum of seventy-two pesos and four reales![26] The disappointment must have intensified his general feeling of disgust with ecclesiastical administration.

Morelos' principal means of supplementing his meager income was to develop a livestock business. Not much in detail is known about this activity, but a letter written to Miguel Cervantes, his brother-in-law, dated October 14, 1810, discloses that Morelos had a large ranch suitable for raising bulls, cows, goats, and hogs, and that he had been able to find buyers for his stock in Valladolid. It had become necessary to augment his income in this way, he explained, because the parochial fees due him were still unpaid, and there had been such a shortage of food that frequently his meals consisted only of corn.[27]

Such was the daily life of the *cura* of Carácuaro, as the monotonous routine of one day gave way to that of another. Apparently Morelos was destined to live out the rest of his time isolated in the remoteness of the *tierra caliente*, outside the main historical stream. Almost surely that would have been his destiny had it not been for one of those strange and sudden developments which can so drastically alter human behavior and patterns of living. On September 16, 1810, Miguel Hidalgo raised the standard of revolt at Dolores. When at length Morelos learned about the aims of the movement, he decided to join. The result for Morelos was a new life and a new career. A priest who otherwise would have remained anonymous thus became a revolutionary who in time would achieve fame and greatness.

REFERENCES

1. H. H. Bancroft, *History of Mexico*, IV, 683.
2. Alejandro de Humboldt, *Ensayo político sobre el Reino de la Nueva España*, II, 133.
3. Edmundo O'Gorman (ed.), "Breve Descripción del Obispado de Michoacán," *Boletín del Archivo General de la Nación*, XI (1940), 136-37.
4. Lillian Estelle Fisher, *Background of the Revolution for Mexican Independence*, p. 239.
5. Bishop Antonio de San Miguel, "Informe del Obispo y Cabildo Eclesiástico de Valladolid de Michoacán al Rey sobre jurisdicción e inmunidades del clero

Americano — 1799," in Alejandro de Humboldt, *Ensayo político sobre el Reino de la Nueva España*, II, 99-103.

6. Morelos to Bishop-elect Abad y Queipo, Carácuaro, June 15, 1810, manuscript in the San Jacinto Museum, San Jacinto Monument, Texas. I have a photostatic copy.

7. Eugenio Reyes Arroyo, "Padrón general de la feligresía de Carácuaro, sus pueblos, y ranchos, y sus haciendas, y estancias por este año de 1798," manuscript in the Archivo del Arzobispado de Valladolid, legajo 736. This archive, located in the north wing of the Casa de Morelos in Morelia, may be the one which James Magner refers to as "the lost archives of the diocese of Michoacán," in his *Men of Mexico*, p. 206. This is a magnificent collection, but the documents still remain in bundles tied with rope, and only a small percentage of the materials have been indexed.

8. Juan José Martínez de Lefarza, *Análisis estadístico de la Provincia de Michoacán en 1822*, p. 122.

9. See, for example, Morelos to José Nazario María de Robles, Carácuaro, April 13, 1807, *Morelos documentos*, II, 255-57.

10. Morelos to Bishop Antonio de San Miguel, Nocupétaro, November 22, 1799, *ibid.*, p. 254.

11. Nicolás Francisco Sausedo to Bishop Antonio de San Miguel, Nocupétaro, undated (1799-?), *ibid.*, pp. 251-53, note 1.

12. Morelos to Bishop Antonio de San Miguel, Nocupétaro, November 22, 1799, *ibid.*, pp. 251-54.

13. Reyes Arroyo to Bishop Antonio de San Miguel, Churumuco, December 16, 1799, Arreguín, *A Morelos*, pp. 38-39.

14. Morelos to Bishop Antonio de San Miguel, Nocupétaro, July 30, 1802, manuscript in Archivo del Arzobispado de Valladolid (legajo is unnumbered). Photostat is in my possession.

15. Morelos to José María de Robles, Carácuaro, April 13, 1807, *Morelos documentos*, II, 255-57.

16. Opinion of Licenciado Miguel Méndez, Valladolid, undated (1807-?), *ibid.*, pp. 257-59.

17. Santiago Camiña to Morelos, Valladolid, July 4, 1807, *ibid.*, pp. 259-60, note 1.

18. Morelos to Juan Antonio de Tapia, Nocupétaro, January 3, 1809, *ibid.*, 258-60.

19. Opinion of Licenciado Francisco de la Concha Castañeda, Valladolid, June 27, 1803, manuscript in Archivo del Arzobispado de Valladolid (legajo unnumbered). Photostat is in my possession.

20. De la Torre, *Bosquejo Histórico*, p. 219.

21. *Ibid.*, p. 220.

22. See document in Alamán, *Historia de Mexico*, IV, appendices, p. 48.

23. Testimony of Morelos, *Morelos documentos*, II, 365.

24. *Ibid.*, III, 13, 31. Nocupétaro is published incorrectly as Querétaro.

25. Teja Zabre, "Posteridad y Presencia de Morelos," *Memoria de la Academia Nacional de Historia y Geografía*, Vol. 1, Año Tercero, Segunda Epoca (1947), pp. 54-55; see also his *Vida de Morelos*, p. 32.

26. Receipt signed by Morelos, Valladolid, October 7, 1809, Guzmán (ed.), *Morelos y la iglesia Católica*, p. 216.

27. Morelos to Miguel Cervantes, Carácuaro, October 14, 1810, *Morelos documentos*, II, 261-62.

CHAPTER III

REVOLUTIONARY
BEGINNINGS

THE invasion of Spain by the French legions of Napoleon Bonaparte in 1808 was the impulse that set into motion a vast revolutionary movement which led ultimately to the overthrow of the Spanish colonial empire in America and the establishment of independent republics throughout all Spanish America. The venal and immoral Manuel Godoy, prime minister in the government of the weak, vacillating Charles IV, and paramour of the queen, had prepared the way for the Napoleonic invasion of Spain. Opposition to the machinations of Godoy had led to the rise of a court faction which had rallied to the support of Prince Ferdinand, Charles' popular son and heir to the throne. After French troops had overrun Portugal late in 1807, and Napoleon had begun to make demands on Godoy and the king for Spanish territory, they decided to flee to America, as the Portuguese royal family had done. When their plan failed, however, Prince Ferdinand had Godoy seized as a traitor. Two days later, on March 19, 1808, King Charles abdicated the throne of Spain, and the prince became King Ferdinand VII.

This factionalism, treachery, and dissension played directly into the hands of the crafty Emperor of the French, who presently persuaded Charles to retract his abdication, invited father and son to Bayonne on French soil, and forced both to renounce all claims to the Spanish throne. Two months later, in July of 1808, Napoleon's brother Joseph was proclaimed King of Spain. The result was resentment and protestation on a national scale, for Spanish subjects everywhere were virtually unanimous in their denunciations of Joseph as a usurper and in their sympathy for the dethroned Ferdinand, who was regarded as the unfortunate victim of Godoy's treachery.[1]

In New Spain the people rallied to the support of the captive Ferdinand and proclaimed their loyalty to him with great enthusiasm. Only the opportunistic Viceroy of New Spain, José de Iturrigaray, was apprehensive, for the fallen Godoy had been his friend and protector. Iturrigaray made no move at first, preferring to watch and wait for a turn of events which he might use to improve his position. Just then the creole-dominated *ayuntamiento,* or municipal council, of Mexico City declared that a protestation of loyalty to Ferdinand should be publicly rendered, but that during his imprisonment, sovereignty should be transferred to the Viceroyalty of New Spain, to be exercised by the *audiencia,* the *ayuntamiento,* and certain other political bodies. The *audiencia,* or supreme judicial power composed of European Spaniards, indicated surprise at the sudden assumption of authority on the part of the *ayuntamiento* and rejected the proposal, thus bringing to life the age-old conflict between creoles and *gachupines* — that is, between American-born and European-born Spaniards.

In the midst of this confused situation Viceroy Iturrigaray concluded finally that his interests would be served best with the convocation of a junta in New Spain patterned after the one that had been established in the peninsula in Seville and which was attempting to govern Spain during the king's absence. Iturrigaray was convinced that such a junta could be controlled easily and that it could be persuaded without too much difficulty to nominate him as king of an independent New Spain. But the plan was detected by the European Spaniards, who saw in it a threat to their position, and who therefore proceeded to form their own plan for the removal of Iturrigaray from office. On September 15, 1808, a group of Spaniards led by Gabriel Yermo seized the viceroy and threw him into prison. The Spanish party in Mexico City then nominated, without official sanction from the Junta of Seville, an old, decrepit soldier named Pedro de Garibay to be Viceroy of New Spain.

Viceroy Garibay, however, was unable to cope with the growing unrest and rising tide of opposition to the Spanish party in Mexico City. When the *audiencia* demanded a replacement, the Junta of Seville in July, 1809, nominated as viceroy the Archbishop of Mexico, Francisco Xavier Lizana y Beaumont. He proved to be no more effective than his predecessor in curbing the growing dissatisfaction, which ripened into open revolt in Valladolid in December, 1809. Organized by José María Obeso, captain of the Valladolid militia, and Fray Vicente de Santa María, a Franciscan, the revolt "was the beginning of armed resistance to Spanish sovereignty in New Spain."[2] It may be added, parenthetically, that the revolt would not end until the independence of Mexico was finally established in 1821.

The conspiracy called for an uprising in the name of Ferdinand VII against the domination of the Spaniards. The support of some 20,000 Indians was sought by promising them the abolition of the tribute. Details concerning the plan of revolt were dispatched to Pátzcuaro, Querétaro, Zitácuaro, and neighboring communities. The entire Intendancy of Guanajuato was to be carried into open rebellion against the ruling authorities of Mexico. The standard of revolt was to be raised on December 21, 1809.

In spite of all precautions taken by the conspirators, their plans became known to the governmental authorities, who moved swiftly to seize its leaders before the revolt could be launched. The viceroy, attempting to conceal his apprehension, then publicly announced there was no cause for alarm. Although the Valladolid plot had miscarried, the viceroy's fears were well founded, as events of the following year proved. The question which should now be asked is with regard to Morelos' connection, if any, with the Valladolid activities. Did he know of plans being formulated? Did he take part in any way? And what effect, if any, did the plot have on him?

No evidence has come to light as yet to indicate that Morelos was in any way connected with the conspiracy at Valladolid or that he took any part in the plans. Since he was in that city on several occasions during 1809, constructing the second story on the house which he had purchased in 1807, and since there is documentary evidence indicating he was there during the last two weeks of September and the first week of October in settling the matter of his inheritance, it is possible he could have heard about, or have known about, or at least have been exposed to the plans being formulated. But if he knew of developments, he apparently took no part; and it is unlikely that they had any great effect on him. Carlos María Bustamante relates, in his usual flamboyant, exaggerated way, that after Morelos heard about the arrest of the conspirators, he "firmly resolved to avenge those great outrages and to make war on the enemies of America." "Deciding to work in any way he could against the Spanish," continues Bustamante, "he began to erect fortifications in his curacy, and to build a crude kind of bulwark by digging a pit between two walls, through the middle of which passed the river. Such were his measures by the time he learned of the Grito de Dolores."[3] But Bustamante has apparently allowed his strong revolutionary partisanship and admiration for Morelos to run away with him, as there is no other evidence that suggests that the year 1810 in the parish of Carácuaro was anything other than normal, at least to mid-October, when Morelos first learned of the Hidalgo movement.

Meanwhile, in the peninsula the courageous struggle of the Spanish guerrillas against the French armies had taken a turn for the worse. The Junta of Seville, driven in 1809 from the mainland to the Isle of León, had become so unpopular that it had taken steps to dissolve itself and transfer its authority to a regency of five members. That body, in turn, then voted to call into session the Cortes, a traditional Spanish representative institution, but failed to provide colonial representation in the Cortes commensurate with a decree of January 22, 1809, which declared that the Spanish dominions overseas were to be considered as integral parts of the Spanish nation. Reluctantly, the regency allowed seven delegates from New Spain to participate in the installation of the Cortes on September 24, 1810, but this concession was hardly enough to quiet opinion in New Spain, which was rapidly moving in the direction of independent thought and action.

In the Viceroyalty of New Spain disgust with the conciliatory policies of Lizana y Beaumont resulted, in February, 1810, in a request for his removal. Accordingly, the Spanish regency appointed as viceroy, Francisco Xavier de Venegas, a distinguished Spanish officer, who assumed the administrative reins in Mexico City on September 14, 1810. Almost immediately he found himself faced with the most formidable revolt Spanish authority in Mexico had yet encountered. The revolutionary flames, which had been so disturbing to Pedro de Garibay and Lizana y Beaumont, and which had never been completely extinguished, had been ignited once again in the Intendency of Guanajuato — this time by the parish priest of Dolores, Miguel Hidalgo.

Miguel Hidalgo y Costilla, the initiator of the Mexican independence movement, was born of creole stock near Pénjamo, in the Intendency of Guanajuato, on May 8, 1753. As a boy he worked on his father's hacienda where he developed an interest in agriculture that remained with him the rest of his life. At the age of fourteen Hidalgo enrolled at San Nicolás College in Valladolid to prepare himself for the priesthood. In 1770 he received the degree of Bachelor of Arts at the Royal and Pontifical University of Mexico, and three years later, a degree in theology from that institution. Some years afterward, though the exact date is uncertain, Hidalgo was ordained a priest.

Hidalgo's brilliant record at San Nicolás enabled him to return there as a member of the faculty, and in subsequent years he taught theology, Latin, and philosophy. In time he became secretary of the college, then vice-rector, and finally rector in 1790. He may have introduced certain unorthodox and prohibited works into the college curriculum, and although there is no evidence that he was censured by the Holy Office, his reforms

so aroused the animosity of his colleagues and the local clergy
that he resigned his position in 1792 to become priest at the
remote little village of Colima. Hidalgo was there only a few
months, however, when he was transferred to the parish of San
Felipe where he remained about ten years. In 1803 he succeeded
his elder brother José Joaquín as *cura* of Dolores, in the northern part of Guanajuato. By that time Hidalgo had fallen under
the suspicious eye of the Inquisition, and was charged with
teaching heretical doctrines, reading prohibited writings, and
advocating French revolutionary ideas. The case against him
was dismissed for lack of evidence; nevertheless, the charges
may have been well founded.

The parish of Dolores, under the guidance of the forceful
and active Father Hidalgo, became much more than just a center for religious activities. His interest in agricultural pursuits
prompted the development of the silk and wine industries,
despite the regulations which outlawed them. A factory for
making pottery and bricks was established, together with a
tannery, carpenter shop, and blacksmith shop. The parish, moreover, was a social and literary center, where creole intellectuals
gathered in the house of the *cura* to discuss the writings of the
18th-century French *philosophes,* and to engage in criticism
and denunciation of the existing political and social system.
Prominent among Hidalgo's associates were Ignacio Allende, a
dashing creole officer and captain of a provincial regiment at
San Miguel el Grande between Dolores and Querétaro, and
Juan Aldama, a lawyer and captain in the San Miguel regiment.
Together with the *corregidor* of Querétaro, Miguel Domínguez,
and his wife, Doña María Josefa Ortiz, Allende and Aldama
were the guiding spirits in the formation of a new plot against
Spanish rule, the center of which was the capital city of Querétaro. It appears that by 1810 Hidalgo was in communication
with the Querétaro group, and was holding frequent conver-
sations with Allende on the progress of the plans.

The objective of the conspiracy was the establishment of a

revolutionary government based on provincial representation which was to rule Mexico in the name of Ferdinand VII but which otherwise was to ignore all allegiance to Spain. A day was set for initiating the revolt, and a general appeal for support was to be directed to all Mexican creoles, Indians, and castes. Every effort was to be made to win over the clergy, but all rich Spaniards and governmental authorities encountered were to be seized. The use of force and violence was to be kept to a minimum, but Allende was to assume command of an insurgent army if strong resistance was met.[4]

There now arises the question of Morelos' involvement, if any, and to what degree, with the Querétaro group preceding the launching of the revolt. Although there has been considerable speculation and controversy among authorities on this point, it is most unlikely that Morelos was involved or was in communication with any of the conspirators, or that he had previous knowledge of their plans. Some writers have fabricated a rather elaborate narrative describing close relations between Hidalgo and Morelos during 1808 and 1809, involving secret correspondence and active plotting for Mexican independence on the part of both men.[5] The source for such an assertion rests solely on a document the authenticity of which was questioned by the Hidalgo scholar José de la Fuente soon after it first came to light in 1908. It purports to be a letter written by Hidalgo to Morelos, dated September 4, 1810, in which Hidalgo confided that he "has just received information from the Center stating that the coming October 29 has been set for the celebration of a great jubilee." He told about the plans being formulated at Querétaro and referred to an interview between Morelos and himself which was held at the end of July. All those who were involved in the plans, such as Mariano Matamoros, said Hidalgo, were highly enthusiastic and confident that the "great jubilee" would be an unqualified success.[6]

When, however, the document in question was subjected to critical analysis, it failed to pass the test. Historian José de la

Fuente presented virtually incontrovertible evidence in support of his contention that the document was a forgery; and it therefore seems fairly safe to conclude that until more trustworthy evidence is produced to prove otherwise, the likelihood of collusion between Morelos and the Querétaro conspiracy of 1810 was extremely remote.

Sometime in August, 1810, the plan of the conspirators became known to the Spanish officials, including the viceroy himself. The story is told that when this information reached the *corregidor*, Miguel Domínguez, he was forced to arrest one of the conspirators. This news was then relayed by the wife of the *corregidor* to Captain Aldama at San Miguel el Grande on the night of September 15. Then in true Paul Revere fashion, Aldama carried the news that night to Allende and Hidalgo, who were in conference at Dolores. According to the story told by Aldama, the *cura* made a hasty decision, sprang to his feet, and exclaimed: "Gentlemen, we are lost; there is no other recourse than to seize the *gachupines* immediately." The household was awakened, and a small group of some twenty men about daybreak ran from door to door spreading the word around the town. Hidalgo addressed the gathering crowd and gave the battle cry that is proclaimed each year throughout Mexico at midnight of September 15-16, and which forever will be remembered in Mexican history as the Grito de Dolores.

The excited mob moved to the jail and forced the officials to free the prisoners. Spaniards were seized. Weapons that could be found were taken and distributed to the crowd. Hidalgo ordered the church bells to be rung, and as the people gathered in anticipation of an earlier mass than usual, their priest addressed them — but there was no mass that day. Instead, Hidalgo exhorted his listeners to recover the lands of their forefathers which the hated Spaniards had stolen three hundred years before, and to overthrow their treacherous Spanish masters who were about to deliver their country and religion to the French. "Defend your rights," shouted Hidalgo. "Long live our

Lady of Guadalupe, long live Ferdinand VII, death to bad government, death to the *gachupines!*"[7]

"The Grito de Dolores had gone forth," Bancroft writes. "The poor and ignorant and down-trodden of this little Indian town proclaim the future independence of a great nation! Enthusiasm rises to religious height, and unarmed as they are, they will follow no matter where, and fight and die no matter how."[8] Hidalgo and the rabble band, with numbers swelled to several thousand, set out for San Miguel el Grande. At Atotonilco a picture of the Virgin of Guadalupe, the patron saint of the Indian population, was taken from the chapel and hoisted to the top of a pole as a symbol of the revolution. San Miguel and Celaya were taken in quick succession, and Guanajuato was subjected to a horrible butchery. As the racial aspects of the movement, Indians versus Spaniards, became more pronounced, protestations of loyalty to Ferdinand became far less meaningful, while "death to the *gachupines*" was understood only as an opportunity for plunder, pillage, and murder.

On October 17 Hidalgo and his army, now increased to 60,000, entered Valladolid, which fell after a feeble resistance. Preparations were now made for an immediate attack on Mexico City. The future success of the revolution seemed assured with the confiscation of 200,000 pesos from the coffers of the cathedral at Valladolid. The army left Valladolid on October 19, passing through Charo, Indaparapeo, and Acambaro. Hidalgo, who had held the title of "Captain-General of America" since the first days of the revolt, was proclaimed Generalissimo on the 22nd. Meanwhile, in Indaparapeo an interview which had an extremely significant effect on the future course of the revolution had been held between two of the greatest personalities the independence movement produced.

Morelos first heard of the Grito de Dolores in the early part of October, 1810. In 1815 he said that he received news in his curacy through Don Rafael Guedea, landlord of the hacienda of Guadalupe, that a revolution had begun in the town of Dolores, and that Cura Don Miguel Hidalgo was at the head of it.[9] This report, however, apparently made no great impression on Morelos, for a letter written on October 14 to his brother-in-law in Valladolid refers to the "flying bullets," but gives no indication that he was particularly concerned about them.[10] A few days later, however, as Hidalgo was about to enter Valladolid, Manuel Abad y Queipo, Bishop-elect of Michoacán, ordered Morelos to publish in his curacy the ban of excommunication of Hidalgo and his followers which had been issued on October 13.[11] No doubt this edict, which condemned the one whom Morelos remembered as his rector at San Nicolás some eighteen years before, aroused his curiosity to the extent that he "felt compelled to go to Hidalgo and talk with him."[12] Moreover, since Morelos had seen some Europeans fleeing from an insurgent army led by his former rector, he decided to take leave of his parish to obtain more information about these developments.[13]

Apparently Morelos' original intention, in the event that he should join with Hidalgo, was to offer his services as a chaplain. He first called on Mariano Escandón y Llera, the Count of Sierragorda, who was the governor of the miter in Valladolid, explaining that he needed a "portable altar," and possibly a replacement for his parish. Escandón at first tried to dissuade Morelos from joining the movement, but failing in this purpose, replied simply that Morelos should try to avoid as much bloodshed as possible, and that a replacement could be obtained by requesting one from his secretary. Morelos then discovered that Hidalgo had already left Valladolid, and so followed him to Charo, overtook him there, and accompanied him to Indaparapeo.[14]

The famous interview between the two men took place on October 20.[15] According to Bustamante, Morelos first offered his services as a chaplain, but Hidalgo, in need of commanders and recognizing a leader when he saw one, persuaded Morelos to take a commission instead.[16] From statements which Morelos made at his trial, together with those contained in a letter he wrote to Hidalgo probably late in 1810, it can be concluded that the interview lasted for several hours, that the two men had a meal together, and that Hidalgo did most of the talking. Asked to give the reason for the edict of excommunication, Hidalgo replied that an explanation was most difficult for him, inasmuch as Spain was in the hands of the French, and the Europeans in Mexico were contriving with the French, preparing to surrender the kingdom, seize the ecclesiastics and church property, and kill all Americans up to a certain age. He insisted that Americans had found themselves with respect to Spain in the same situation as those Spaniards in the peninsula who opposed French rule. Hidalgo added that the objective of the revolt was independence, that the king's absence from Spain had occasioned it, and that all Americans who wished to join in an effort to save kingdom and religion could do so. Morelos replied that he agreed with the arguments, and that at one time he had heard some lawyers say that a kingdom should be returned to its own people in case its king was absent. Hidalgo then wrote out the following orders: "For the present, I commission in due form Señor Don José María Morelos, Cura of Carácuaro, as my *lugar-teniente* and order him to proceed to the south coast, raise troops, and carry out the verbal instructions which I have given him." These instructions included the collection of arms, reorganization of the government, seizure of Europeans, deportation of their families, confiscation of their property, and, above all, the capture of Acapulco.[17]

Morelos returned immediately to Valladolid. When he failed to find Escandón y Llera, the governor of the miter, he left a note explaining that he had tried to find Escondón since early in the morning, but having no time to lose, since he had been commissioned to go to the south coast, he felt obliged to leave a note requesting a replacement for his parish. The next day the secretary appointed José María Méndez to Morelos' parish and gave instructions that notice of the appointment be communicated to Morelos through his brother-in-law, Miguel Cervantes.[18]

Why then, it may be asked, did Morelos rather suddenly

decide to break with his past, to abandon the relatively quiet and peaceful life of the parish priest, to embark upon a career of a revolutionary and military commander leading forces against the ruling authorities? The answer would seem to involve a complex set of attitudes, motives, influences, and various other forces which may have been at work. His experience at Carácuaro was hardly a pleasant or satisfying one. Morelos must have felt a growing sense of futility, frustration, and hopelessness, and he may have decided by 1810 that if he was to make a significant contribution in his lifetime he would have to look in another direction. He must have become dissatisfied with, and even resentful of, Spanish officialdom, whether civil or ecclesiastical; and he must have been distrustful of Europeans generally. Thus, Hidalgo's personality, persuasiveness, and explanation of his movement struck a responsive chord, and transformed thoughts, feelings, and attitudes which Morelos had been harboring for some time into revolutionary activity. Hidalgo had convinced Morelos that "his obligation to the party of independence was greater than that to his parish." Morelos joined the revolution, therefore, because "Cura Hidalgo, who had been his rector, said that the cause was just."[19]

REFERENCES

1. This background material has been taken largely from H. H. Bancroft, *History of Mexico*, IV, 22-96; and H. I. Priestley, *The Mexican Nation*, 196-206.
2. *Ibid.*, p. 203; see also Juan E. Hernández y Dávalos (ed.), *Colección de documentos para la historia de la guerra de independencia de Mexico de 1808 á 1821*, II, 5.
3. Carlos Bustamante, *Cuadro histórico*, I, 19; II, 3.
4. The background of the Hidalgo movement has been taken from Bancroft, *History of Mexico*, IV, 107-290; John Anthony Caruso, *The Liberators of Mexico*, pp. 3-35; and James Magner, *Men of Mexico*, pp. 206-212.
5. Alejandro Villaseñor y Villaseñor, *Biografías de los héroes y caudillos de la independencia*, II, 38; Victor Esperon, *Morelos*, pp. 43-44.
6. Published in facsimile in *El Imparcial*, September 11, 1908. I have a photostatic copy. See also José de la Fuente, "Un autógrafo de Hidalgo," *Boletín de la Sociedad de Geografía y Estadística*, III, 41-53.
7. Hugh M. Hamill, Jr., "Early Psychological Warfare in the Hidalgo Revolt," *Hispanic American Historical Review*, XLI (May, 1961), 206-207.
8. Bancroft, *History of Mexico*, IV, 117-18.
9. Testimony of Morelos, *Morelos documentos*, II, 331.

10. Morelos to Miguel Cervantes, Carácuaro, October 14, 1810, *ibid.*, II, 261-62.
11. Testimony of Morelos, *ibid.*, III, 17.
12. *Ibid.*, II, 332.
13. *Ibid.*, pp. 331-32.
14. *Ibid.*, III, 27; II, 331.
15. (Morelos ?) to Hidalgo, undated (November, 1810 ?), *ibid.*, II, 263.
16. Bustamante, *Cuadro histórico*, I, 73.
17. Testimony of Morelos, *Morelos documentos*, III, 30-31; II, 332.
18. Morelos to Ramón Aguilar, Valladolid, October 21, 1810, *ibid.*, II, 262; Order of Ramón Francisco de Aguilar, Valladolid, October 22, 1810, *ibid.*, 262-63, note 1.
19. Testimony of Morelos, *ibid.*, III, 27.

CHAPTER IV

SPREADING THE REVOLUTION

HAVING been commissioned as *lugar-teniente* by Miguel Hidalgo for the conquest of the Pacific coast and the fortress of Acapulco, Morelos set out from Carácuaro, on October 25, 1810, with approximately a score of poorly armed volunteers.[1] The task which lay ahead was stupendous. For the time being at least, his personal qualities of leadership, his knowledge of the terrain of the *tierra caliente*, and the possible advantage of surprise would have to compensate for his complete lack of military experience and lack of an army, ammunition, and supplies even in their most elementary form. Yet within three weeks' time, the small band moved rapidly through Churumuco and Coahuayutla, and, gathering men and weapons as it advanced, passed on to Zacatula on the coast, and then moved rapidly down the coast through Petatlán, Tecpán, El Zanjón, and Coyuca. Little resistance was encountered, and such opposition as the royalists could offer was swept aside, all weapons and booty of the enemy being seized. On November 12 Morelos' army, numbering more than two thousand men and in possession of several cannon, occupied the town of Aguacatillo, on the outskirts of Acapulco.[2]

The port of Acapulco, situated on the west side of a magnificent harbor, and well known to travelers from both the United States and Mexico, had been for years one of the strongest garrisons in colonial New Spain. The surrounding towns of El Veladero, La Sabana, Las Cruces, Llano Largo, and Marqués could be garrisoned in case of attack from the land side, and thus served as an outer defense system for the port. The inner defense system was built around a fortress castle, which was situated on the east side of the harbor and was reported to be so impregnable that it could resist a siege indefinitely, provided the supply lines leading to it could be maintained. The famous Anglo-American adventurer and soldier-of-fortune Peter Ellis Bean, who had just escaped from a Spanish prison there as Morelos' army entered the area, wrote that the fortress castle was built of stone with walls twelve feet thick and had about a hundred guns of the largest caliber.[3] Storming and taking this strong point was the task that lay ahead for Morelos and his newly assembled, inexperienced, untried, out-numbered army.

An attempt of the insurgents to scale El Veladero heights on November 13 took an unexpected turn. Since both insurgents and royalists were inexperienced in combat, they ran at the sight of each other, fleeing from the field. Within a few days, however, the desertion of many royalists to the insurgent forces permitted Morelos to occupy the strategically important towns of El Veladero and La Sabana, giving his insurgents a commanding position over the port and enabling them to disrupt the royalist line of communications with the capital. Morelos wrote Hidalgo that he was preparing to lay siege to the fortress, since he lacked sufficient men and ammunition for an immediate and all-out assault.[4] Although royalist reinforcements attempted to dislodge the insurgents from their hold on Aguacatillo, Morelos anticipated the move, and on January 4, 1811, won a resounding victory at Tres Palos, capturing a vast quantity of military stores.[5] While Morelos called on the nearby haciendas and villages for men and money, Viceroy Xavier Venegas, who by this time had become thoroughly familiar with the name "Morelos" through the dispatches he had received from his commander at Acapulco, sent additional reinforcements to the royalists. The result was a prolonged stalemate of almost six months' duration.

Both sides resorted to every kind of trickery and device to resolve the deadlock. Morelos conducted clandestine negotiations with a royalist artillery officer named Pepe Gago whereby the fortress was to be surrendered to the insurgents in accordance with a certain prearranged signal. The night of February 7,

Morelos and his army advanced from La Sabana and took a position at Las Iguanas. At four o'clock in the morning the insurgents sighted the signal and advanced toward the fortress in two columns. As they came within range, the guns of the fortress and those of the ships in the harbor released a tremendous volley of fire, whereupon Morelos quickly withdrew to Las Iguanas and laid siege. For nine days he kept up a steady fire, but on February 19, when a royalist sortie captured the greater part of his artillery, he fell back to La Sabana.[6] Since Morelos was no longer able to prevent the arrival of royalist reinforcements or to interrupt the flow of supplies which were brought in by sea from San Blas, he decided early in May to abandon the attack altogether. Leaving a small force on the El Veladero heights to watch the movement of the royalists, he set out with the main body of his army through the mountain passes to the north.[7]

On May 22 at the hacienda of Chichihualco, Morelos defeated a royalist force and two days later entered Chilpancingo. On the 26th he took Tixtla, where eight cannon and two hundred muskets were captured. Here he remained for two months, strengthening the town's fortifications, enlisting volunteers, appointing commanders, and drilling his men. On August 15 Morelos successfully repulsed a royalist attack, and three days later his forces entered Chilapa, where he remained until the following November.[8] The capture of Chilapa marked the end of what is generally referred to as Morelos' first campaign, and terminated one year of military operations. Within that time, though the injunction of Hidalgo to capture Acapulco had not been carried out, effective fighting forces had been organized and trained, and strict disciplinary requirements instituted; the major part of the southern coast had been brought under insurgent control; and a deep wedge had been driven into the area to the north between the Sierra Madres and the capital.

During this time a number of outstanding figures rallied to the banner of Morelos. They not only served with distinction as commanders of Morelos' armies, but also held high office and positions of responsibility, years later, after independence was established. Earliest among the group to offer his services was Hermenegildo Galeana, born of an *hacendado* family of the Tecpán area and grandson of an English buccaneer named Galen who had been shipwrecked on the Pacific coast in the early part of the eighteenth century, and who had settled down to become a prosperous cotton planter. Though illiterate, Galeana possessed exceptional ability and was among the ablest of Morelos' officers. At length he gave his life for the cause in a battle near Coyuca in June, 1814.[9]

The Bravo family was living on the hacienda of Chichihualco when the movement for independence began. The family repeatedly rejected demands of the royalists to take up arms in defense of the government; and when a company of royalists seized and occupied all the haciendas in the Chilpancingo area, the Bravos fled and hid in a cave for several months. According to Carlos María Bustamante, when they received a letter from Morelos inviting them to join his army, they responded by attaching themselves to Galeana's force, which had entered the area in May, 1811.[10] From that time on, five Bravos — Leonardo and his brothers Miguel, Victor, and Maximo, and Leonardo's son Nicolás — served the insurgent cause with distinction, and two of these men laid down their lives. Of the five, Nicolás was the most important, both during the struggle for independence and in the period immediately after it was achieved.

The name of Vicente Guerrero may also be counted among those great leaders who served Morelos and received their first military training from him. Born of humble origins in the Tixtla area, Guerrero probably joined Morelos in 1810. After Morelos' death in 1815, he became the recognized commander-in-chief of the insurgent forces and the heir to the Hidalgo-Morelos program of reform. With the royalist commander Agustín Iturbide, Guerrero negotiated the celebrated Plan de Iguala of February 24, 1821, which called for the independence of Mexico, though on terms vastly different from those Morelos had envisaged. Guerrero later became constitutional president of the Mexican nation.[11]

Perhaps the ablest of Morelos' commanders, with the possible exception of Hermenegildo Galeana, was Mariano Matamoros. He was serving as *cura* of Jantetelco in the jurisdiction of Cuernavaca when the revolution broke out, but left his curacy to join the insurgent cause as Morelos' force neared Izúcar. He rose rapidly because of his fighting ability, becoming in July, 1813 a *teniente-general* and second in command to Morelos. In early 1814 he was captured, given a speedy trial, and executed on February 3 in Valladolid.[12]

Another name deserving mention among those who served under the leadership of Morelos and who attained prominence in Mexican politics later was Manuel Félix Fernández, better known by his impressive pseudonym, Guadalupe Victoria. He was an able leader and a man of great courage; more than once he saved Morelos' life. He went into hiding after Morelos' death, when the revolution was all but extinguished. He survived somehow and later became the first constitutional president of the Mexican republic.[13]

One Anglo-American, Peter Ellis Bean, should be included among those who joined the Morelos movement during its first year of military operations and who contributed significantly to the cause. Soldier-of-fortune and cosmopolitan adventurer, Bean had come to Mexico as a member of the ill-fated Philip Nolan expedition that entered Texas in 1800. Taken captive and imprisoned by Spanish authorities, Bean escaped as Morelos entered the Acapulco area, joined his insurgent army, and aided the revolutionaries immeasurably through his knowledge of the manufacture of gunpowder. "As there were large quantities of saltpeter in the country," wrote Bean, "and I was the only one who understood the manufacture of powder, I set up a powder mill. We obtained sulphur from a mine near Chilpancingo, and while the Indian women ground the material on their *metates*,

I made the powder."[14] Bean remained with Morelos until 1814, when he was sent to the United States to obtain aid for the insurgent cause.[15]

In building an effective fighting force Morelos believed that a well-drilled, disciplined army of between two and three thousand, which could be trained to strike hard and fast, move quickly, harass the enemy, and make the fullest use of guerrilla tactics, would be far more productive of results than a large, unruly, unmanageable mob, such as Hidalgo used. Morelos felt that promotion should be based on performance and merit. Officers who lacked leadership and courage, or who permitted their men to plunder, he regarded as unfit for responsibility. Such were to be deprived of their commands and sent home. Morelos also prescribed the death penalty for anyone, officer or enlisted man, found guilty of insubordination, disobedience, cowardice, treason, "or any disturbance which is opposed to the law of God, the peace of the kingdom, and the progress of our arms."[16]

Evidence that Morelos meant what he said about treasonable activity within the ranks of the insurgent forces was his handling of the so-called David-Tabares affair. In early summer, 1811, Morelos commissioned two men to undertake a trip to the north for the purpose of negotiating a treaty of alliance with the United States. One was David Faro, a survivor like Peter Ellis Bean of the Nolan expedition; the other was a man named Mariano Tabares. On the way north they were stopped by Ignacio López Rayón, who explained that he had assumed the headship of the Hidalgo insurrection, inasmuch as royalist forces had captured that leader. Rayón gave both men commissions, but he ordered them to return to the south. At Chilapa, Faro and Tabares encountered Morelos, who refused to recognize their commissions, whereupon the two men, disappointed and despondent, retired to El Veladero and made plans to incite the Negroes in Morelos' army to slaughter the whites. When Morelos heard about this activity, he struck hard and fast. Taking a small escort with him, he rushed southward to "remove the cancer," crushed the revolt before it could be launched, and caught and shot the leaders.[17]

Reporting on the progress of his military operations, Morelos wrote in August, 1811, that he had four batallions under arms — one protecting the coastal ports, one at El Veladero outside Acapulco, and one each at Tixtla and Chilpancingo, guarding the gunpowder supply and making preparations for continuing the campaign.

I place my confidence in these troops, [he said] for they have been selected with my approval. . . . Supporting our cause are the natives of fifty towns. They number several thousand, and while they are not disciplined, they can serve well in a subordinate capacity. I have therefore sent these men back to their fields for the purpose of sustaining the troops. I have a corresponding number under arms and more than fifty cannon of various calibers. I have hurled forth my call to freedom in Cuautla de Amilpas, Puebla, and Oaxaca; and since these towns will respond immediately when the cultivation of the fields is completed, I have no doubt about the progress of our movement in those provinces.[18]

For the purpose of financing the insurgent military effort Morelos decreed in November, 1810, that in the area lying under his control the tobacco monopoly and the *alcabala,* or sales tax, would continue in force. An American (Mexican) was to be under no obligation to pay a debt owed to a European, but those debts owed by Europeans to Americans were to be collected immediately.[19] Moreover, Morelos called upon the wealthy landowners for contributions and loans, and exhorted the people to give as much as they could. Tax officials were appointed to collect existing governmental revenues for financing the revolution; and all goods, arms, provisions, and properties that belonged to Europeans were to be confiscated and used to support the insurgent armies.[20] Steps were taken to provide a new currency, with the issuance of copper coins which were to serve as a temporary medium of exchange, to be redeemable later at face value in gold or silver currency. Sufficient quantities of copper were available to the insurgent government in the Tecpán area, but copper was the only metal used at first for coinage purposes in view of the scarcity of all other metals.[21] Morelos also made an effort to improve the communications of the insurgents when he established on September 15, 1811, a mail service connecting Chilapa with Pátzcuaro, and the latter with Zitácuaro, where Ignacio Rayón had set up a revolutionary government. The mail facilities would be expanded, Morelos declared, as the revolution progressed.[22]

While organizing an effective fighting machine and conquering the greater part of the southern coast and south-central interior, Morelos was forging a far-reaching program of political and social reform. At Aguacatillo on November 17, 1810, less than a month after he began his first campaign, he proclaimed what he called "a new government, by which all inhabitants, except *gachupines,* [would] no longer be designated as Indians, mulattoes, or castes, but all [would be] known as Americans." In the same proclamation he decreed the abolition of slavery, of the tribute, and of communal treasury chests. The Indians were to retain the income from the lands on which they lived and worked.[23] As a recent author has written, "It was one of the most important documents in the social history of Latin America."[24] The revolution was justified, Morelos insisted, because the perfidious *gachupines* were the enemies of mankind, who for three centuries had enslaved and subjugated the native population, stifled the natural development of the kingdom, squandered its wealth and resources, and violated the sacred cult. Now since Spain was in the hands of the French, Morelos declared, and the *gachupines* were conspiring with Bonaparte to perpetuate their power, all Americans must unite in defense of country and religion.[25]

Morelos made a special appeal to the creoles. Those who would cooperate and support the movement would be entrusted with positions of the greatest responsibility in the government and in the army, and their property and wealth would be respected. On the other hand, those creoles who were reluctant to join with the insurgents were to be treated as *gachupines,* liable to a firing squad if captured, and their property was to be confiscated.[26]

With regard to the situation in Spain, Morelos made his position clear. "Now there is no Spain," he wrote in 1811, "because the French are in control of it. There is no Ferdinand VII, because either he went to France voluntarily (and in that case, we are not obligated to recognize him as king), or he was carried away by force and no longer exists as king. Even if he should be living, it is lawful for a conquered kingdom to be reconquered, and for an obedient kingdom to repudiate a king when he is so oppressive with his laws that they become intolerable."[27] At another time Morelos made the point that since Ferdinand was a prisoner in France and at the mercy of the despotic Bonaparte, the inhabitants of New Spain were justified in ruling themselves, because "when kings are absent, sovereignty resides in the nation, which is free to form the type of government which it desires. No nation is obligated to remain a slave of another."[28]

The source for these interesting political and social ideas was most likely Miguel Hidalgo. The Hidalgo movement late in 1810 was strongly inclined to place a greater emphasis on independence and less on Ferdinand VII. Also there was a striking coincidence between the respective social programs of Hidalgo and Morelos, both as to content and timing. Yet there was considerable originality in Morelos' program, the most conspicuous feature being his novel use of the term "American," with a new emphasis on nationality as the chief criterion for an individual's place in the new order, instead of racial composition or social status. Moreover, there would be noticeably more originality and independence in Morelos' thought as the fortunes of the Hidalgo revolution declined in 1811. Because Morelos emphasized the role of the native-born, and did not allow his movement to degenerate into that of an undisciplined Indian horde as Hidalgo had permitted his, respectable Mexican creoles found the program of Morelos much more attractive than that of Hidalgo.

There was also the painful and delicate subject of Morelos' relations with the Church and the problem of reconciling the revolution with religion. Since Church and State were so inextricably linked in the Spanish colonial system, a priest who took up arms against the government would inevitably be charged with heresy. Thus, the bishop of Oaxaca in 1811 exhorted his parishioners to defend their persons, lives, and treasures from the bandit army commanded by the "traitorous and sacrilegious Morelos," whose desire was to "profane the sacred faith and introduce confusion, disorder, and tyranny."[29] Morelos' reply was that he had no quarrel with religion; that the revolution was actually being waged in defense of it; that the conflict was motivated not by any controversy over dogma or doctrine but only by a sincere desire to free Mexico from the political, social, and economic domination of the Europeans, who had usurped the rights of the people for so long.[30] And so the controversy raged. It was not the first time by any means that Morelos was involved in a dispute with the ecclesiastical authorities, nor was it his last.

A recent investigation of the role of the clergy in the movement for Mexican independence indicates that the upper clergy were to a large extent loyal to the established system and opposed to independence, while the lower clergy divided sharply in their reactions to the rebellion. Many of the latter remained loyal, and a majority were probably neutral in the struggle; yet an important segment joined the insurrection and played a role of greater significance than their numbers would indicate. They filled the military commands, contributed greatly to activities concerned with press and propaganda, and soothed the consciences of their ignorant countrymen when the decree of excommunication was hurled against them. "Had the lower clergy opposed *en masse*," says a recent study, "the rebellion of 1810 would have been only a minor affair, and the whole course of the Mexican movement for independence would have been changed."[31]

One of the harshest denunciations Morelos received came from the pen of Manuel Ignacio Campillo, Bishop of Puebla, native of that city and the only creole bishop in New Spain, in a letter, dated November 14, 1811. "Your conduct," wrote the bishop, "is certainly not that of a priest of the New Testament. Instead of leading souls to heaven, you are sending thousands to hell." He then accused Morelos of having imprisoned and mistreated various fellow priests, of administering the sacraments and making appointments without the bishop's permission, and of adding sacrilege to bloodshed. The bishop continued:

When I try to calculate the crimes provoked by the insurgents, my imagination is overwhelmed, and I see only an ocean of crime and sin, in which you are submerged. . . . What if you succeed in all your plans? What if you establish the independence of America? What if you finish with the Europeans and make this realm the most prosperous empire in the world? What will all these advantages and this glory serve you in the next life? In that place, political considerations and temporal advantages mean nothing.

When you are locked up in a jail and are about to ascend an ignominious scaffold like Hidalgo, or when you are stretched out upon a bed a few moments before you take your last breath, you will see the horror of the deeds which you are now committing, although you do not now recognize them because of the blindness which the exaltation of your passions has wrought upon your reason.[32]

In his reply, Morelos declared that the clergy he had imprisoned had been confined only because of their opposition to the revolution, and that they were receiving good treatment. The sacraments, he said, were being administered only in cases of necessity, and marriages were still awaiting the episcopal dispensation. He added that one of his most bitter enemies, Manuel Abad y Queipo, Bishop-elect of Michoacán, had granted dispensations to the insurgents of Atoyac. He continued:

Your Excellency has declared that independence is still a political problem, and I should add that the necessary means for prosecuting the present war can also be defended on this hypothesis. Would to

God that Your Excellency might take up the pen to defend it in favor of the Americans! You would, without doubt, find greater reasons for it than that of the Anglo-Americans or the people of Isreal. The justice of our cause is *per se nota.* . . .The truth is, Illustrious Sir, that Your Excellency has done us small favor in your manifestoes, for in them you have done nothing more than to blacken our conduct, conceal our rights, and praise the Europeans — a great dishonor to the nation and its armies. . . . For myself, it would be easier to apply to Rome for a dispensation after the war than to survive the guillotine, and to preserve religion with more purity among my countrymen than among the French and other foreigners. The people will not lay down their arms until the task is done.[33]

Thus, religion, while serving as the instrument of both parties and their causes, was not in itself an issue. Morelos had no quarrel with the Catholic church, its hierarchical system, or its doctrine. As a matter of fact, he considered himself as playing a role of champion and defender of the faith. His attack was directed against the European clergy. The basis of his rebellion against their authority was political, social, and national, rather than religious. Almost all members of the lower clergy who joined and participated in the struggle for independence viewed the issue of revolution and religion in the same light.

REFERENCES

1. Testimony of Morelos, *Morelos documentos,* II, 333; III, 12.
2. *Ibid.,* II, 333; Rafael Aguirre Colorado et al., *Campañas de Morelos sobre Acapulco,* pp. 12-13.
3. "Memoir of Ellis P. Bean," in H. Yoakum, *History of Texas,* I, 419.
4. (Morelos) to Hidalgo, undated and unsigned, *Morelos documentos,* II, 263.
5. Testimony of Morelos, *ibid.,* p. 335.
6. *Ibid.,* p. 336.
7. *Ibid.,* p. 337.
8. *Ibid.,* p. 338.
9. Alejandro Villaseñor y Villaseñor, *Biografías de los héroes y caudillos de la independencia,* II, 47, 54.
10. Bustamante, *Cuadro histórico,* II, 15.
11. See William Forrest Sprague, *Vicente Guerrero, Mexican Liberator—A Study in Patriotism,* pp. 16-17.
12. See José de la Fuente, "Matamoros," *Anales del Museo Nacional de Arqueología Historia y Etnología,* Ser. 3, Vol. IV (1912), 302-303; José de Coéllar (ed.), *Proceso del caudillo de la independencia Don Mariano Matamoros,* pp. 9, 10, 31.

13. Manuel Rivera Cambas, *Los gobernantes de México*, II, 111.

14. "Memoir of Ellis P. Bean," in Yoakum, *History of Texas*, I, 440; Bean to Morelos, Chilpancingo, January 11, 1812, Archivo General de la Nación, Sección de Historia, Operaciones de Guerra, Morelos, tomo VI; Bennett Lay, *The Lives of Ellis P. Bean*, pp. 75-76; 79.

15. "Memoir of Ellis P. Bean," in Yoakum, *History of Texas*, I, 446.

16. Decree of Morelos, Tecpán, October 13, 1811, Hernández y Dávalos (ed.), *Colección*, III, 402.

17. Testimony of Morelos, *Morelos documentos*, II, 335.

18. Morelos to Ignacio Rayón, Tixtla, August 13, 1811, *ibid.*, I, 126.

19. Decree of Morelos, Aguacatillo, November 17, 1810, *ibid.*, I, 123.

20. Decree of Morelos, Izúcar, December 13, 1811, Hernández y Dávalos (ed.), *Colección*, III, 450.

21. Decree of Morelos, Tixtla, July 13, 1811, *Morelos documentos*, I, 124; Alberto Francisco Pradeau, *Numismatic History of Mexico*, p. 101.

22. Decree of Morelos, Chilapa, September 15, 1811, Hernández y Dávalos (ed.), *Colección*, III, 376.

23. Decree of Morelos, Aguacatillo, November 17, 1810, *Morelos documentos*, I, 123.

24. John Anthony Caruso, *The Liberators of Mexico*, p. 90.

25. Proclamation of Morelos, *Morelos documentos*, I, 132-33.

26. Decree of Morelos, Tecpán, October 13, 1811, Hernández y Dávalos (ed.), *Colección*, III, 402; Proclamation of Morelos, *Morelos documentos*, I, 138.

27. Decree of Morelos, *ibid.*, p. 139.

28. Proclamation of Morelos, *ibid.*, p. 141.

29. Proclamation of the Bishop of Oaxaca, August 26, 1811, Hernández y Dávalos (ed.), *Colección*, V, 904.

30. Morelos to the *Cura* of Tuzantla, Chilapa, (September ?), 22, 1811, José María Morelos Papers, 1795-1815, Genaro García Collection, Latin American Collection, University of Texas. Hereafter cited as Morelos Papers, LAC UT. Unless otherwise indicated, manuscripts cited from the Latin American Collection of the University of Texas are to be found in the Genaro García Collection.

31. Karl M. Schmitt, "The Clergy and the Independence of New Spain," *Hispanic American Historical Review*, XXXIV (August, 1954), 311.

32. Bishop Manuel Ignacio Campillo to Morelos, Puebla, November 14, 1811, Hernández y Dávalos (ed.), *Colección*, III, 468-69; quoted in James Magner, *Men of Mexico*, pp. 245-46.

33. Morelos to Bishop Campilla, Tlapa, November 24, 1811, Hernández y Dávalos (ed.), *Colección*, III, 483-86.

CHAPTER V

THE RAYON MOVEMENT

WHILE Morelos was engaged in organizing an insurgent army and spreading the revolution in the south, important developments were taking place in the region to the north involving the fortunes of the initiator of independence, Miguel Hidalgo. His army, it will be remembered, had left Valladolid in the latter part of October, 1810, with Mexico City as its objective. There was still much confusion within insurgent ranks as to the motive of the revolt, but there was a tendency to emphasize independence more and Ferdinand VII less as the movement progressed; in fact, for a while both were proclaimed simultaneously![1]

To check the advance of Hidalgo, Viceroy Venegas, concerned as much about his head as his office, dispatched the loyal but unpopular royalist commander, Torcuato Trujillo. The two armies met at Monte de las Cruces and in the terrifying battle which followed, Trujillo suffered such heavy losses that he was forced to retreat to the capital. Although he claimed a great victory, his reception was noticeably lacking in enthusiasm, and the viceroy seriously contemplated flight to Vera Cruz. On the other hand Hidalgo gave the order to retreat, although Allende strongly urged that the march on the capital be pressed. The usual explanation, and the one Hidalgo gave to Rayón, is that he had decided that his own forces were inadequate for the penetration of the capital's defenses, in view of the heavy losses of personnel and military equipment at Monte de las Cruces. But Hidalgo had told Morelos that although his ammunition supply was depleted, there would be "no delay in approaching Mexico City with forces that would make the enemy tremble."[2]

While the battle of Monte de las Cruces was being fought,

a royalist force under the command of Félix María Calleja occupied Querétaro. Calleja, who would become Morelos' foremost adversary as a royalist commander and later as successor to Viceroy Venegas, was arrogant, suspicious, vain, ruthless, cruel, but easily the most competent and effective of the viceroy's generals. Ordered by Venegas to reinforce the capital's defenses, Calleja set out by way of Aculco, while Hidalgo was falling back to the same place, not knowing that the royalists had recaptured Querétaro. The two armies, ignorant of the other's approach, met near Aculco on November 6, and the royalists won a decisive victory. The insurgents retreated to Guadalajara, while Calleja entered Guanajuato, where in characteristic fashion he made the most determined effort to avenge Hidalgo's slaughter of Spaniards two months before.

At Guadalajara, Hidalgo proclaimed several reforms and undertook the organization of a revolutionary government. In a series of decrees issued in late November and early December, 1810, he emancipated the slaves, abolished the tribute, restored communal lands to the Indians, prohibited pillage, removed existing restrictions on the production of wine and tobacco, and imposed a tax on certain agricultural products to obtain revenue for the revolutionary government. Two ministerial posts were created: José María Chico, a young Guanajuato lawyer, was appointed head of the department of justice, and Ignacio Rayón, Hidalgo's personal secretary, became secretary of state. For the dissemination of information and propaganda, an insurgent paper was established, *El Despertador Americano;* and Pascasio Ortiz de Letona was appointed as envoy plenipotentiary to the United States to seek aid and treaties of alliance and commerce. Unfortunately for the insurgent cause, Letona was apprehended before he left the country and took poison to escape execution.

Receiving information on January 13, 1811, that an army under Calleja was approaching Guadalajara, Hidalgo organized his defenses outside the city at the bridge of Calderón. The two armies met in a great battle, described as one "between quantity and quality, between courage and discipline, between heart and head."[3] On several occasions it appeared that victory was within grasp of the insurgents, but when a fire accidentally broke out in the midst of their ranks, the entire army, terrified and panic-stricken, fled in the utmost confusion and disorder. "It was an accident," says Bancroft, "which overruled the power of battle and held back the cause of independence for eleven tedious and bloody years."[4] Calleja entered Guadalajara in triumph, and Hidalgo and the remnants of his army fled to the north.

As the broken insurgent army retreated northward, the breach which had been developing slowly but steadily between Hidalgo and Allende broke into the open. Hidalgo was forced to transfer his authority to Allende, who led the retreating army through Saltillo northward in the direction of Monclova. On the morning of March 21 as the group trudged onward toward Texas, it was suddenly set upon by a force commanded by Ignacio Elizondo, who only recently had betrayed the insurgents because of a quarrel with Allende, and all of the leaders were captured, including Hidalgo himself. "Never was a plot more perfidiously planned or more successfully accomplished."[5]

The captive insurgents were led over the long, dusty trail to Chihuahua, where they were given a speedy trial, condemned, and, with the exception of one prisoner who received life imprisonment, all were sentenced to die. Hidalgo conducted himself with extreme dignity and fortitude throughout the agonizing proceedings before the civil and ecclesiastical author-ities, and assumed full responsibility for leading the insurrection. He declared that his purpose was the independence of Mexico, and that he was attempting to preserve its institutions from the French. He never had an opportunity to devise a form of govern-ment, he said, and he was still a devout Roman Catholic, as he had always been. But before the military court could pass sentence, canonical law required that he must first be degraded from the priesthood. On July 29 the ceremony of degradation was performed, and shortly after, the sentence of death was pronounced against him. Two days later a firing squad carried out the order. The authenticity of the recantation supposedly written by Hidalgo in which he sought forgiveness for the evil, the destruction, and the bloodshed he had caused, is still a subject of debate; and the truth about Hidalgo's sentiments during his last days may never be known. His revolution accomplished but little, because his talents and genius lay in the realm of the idealistic, the emotional, and the inspirational, rather than in the practical, the administrative, or the military. But as the initiator of the movement which subsequently brought independence, his claim to the title of "Father of Mexican Independence" is fully deserved. It has been said that without Hidalgo there would have been no Agustín Iturbide; for strangely enough, although he helped defeat Hidalgo, by a peculiar turn of events he later effected the independence of Mexico which Hidalgo initiated. It may be added that without Hidalgo there would have been no Morelos.

After the capture and execution of Hidalgo and his associates, the leadership of the movement passed to Ignacio López Rayón, a man of moderate attainment, but lacking Hidalgo's idealism and humanitarianism and Morelos' qualities of leadership and devotion. Born in Tlalpujahua, Michoacán, in 1773, Rayón studied philosophy in Valladolid and received a law degree from the College of San Ildefonso in Mexico City. For a short time he practiced law, but was engaged in mining operations near the town of his birth when he joined the Hidalgo movement soon after the Grito.[6] He became Hidalgo's personal secretary and fought in all major engagements against the royalists. Elevated to the position of secretary of state, Rayón apparently was the originator of the idea of the Letona mission. As the Hidalgo group retreated northward from Guadalajara, a special military tribunal of the principal insurgent officers met in Saltillo and appointed Rayón commander-in-chief, while the others departed on a journey to the United States in search of aid and supplies.[7] But with the news of the capture of the insurgent leaders and the approach of royalist forces, Rayón abandoned Saltillo, and at length, after a long and difficult march, he and his force arrived at Zacatecas, where he began organizing a provincial government, training soldiers, and extracting metals from the nearby mines.

From that point, apparently in the hope of effecting a reconciliation with Calleja, Rayón and his second-in-command, José María Liceaga, wrote a letter to the royalist commander on April 22, 1811, explaining the nature and motive of the insurgent revolution, and inviting his support and cooperation in the establishment of a national junta. It was to be modeled after the one in the peninsula: it would govern the country in the name of Ferdinand VII, and would protect the kingdom and its institutions from French conquest.[8] Calleja, however, flatly rejected the offer, replying that he would not welcome further communications from the insurgents. The only basis for reconciliation acceptable to him, he explained, was for the insurgents to surrender all arms, ammunition, and funds, and receive the benefits of a general pardon. These conditions Rayón refused. As he heard of Calleja's approach, he evacuated Zacatecas, retired southward to the mountain retreat of Zitácuaro, which lay about midway between Valladolid and Mexico City, and proceeded during the summer of 1811 with the organization of his national junta.

On July 13 Rayón wrote Morelos, explaining the need for greater cooperation among the insurgent chiefs and the desirability of centralizing authority for checking the anarchy which prevailed. Such ends could be accomplished, Rayón pointed out, through the formation of a national junta, which would unify and coordinate the insurgent effort. Morelos, having received news of Hidalgo's capture through intercepted letters, and likewise seeing the need for centralized authority, replied to Rayón that he was in accord. "It appears that we are of the same opinion," wrote Morelos, "on the formation of the junta. . . . No doubt in the beginning of the struggle it was necessary to hand out numerous commissions to augment the leaven, but it is now time to knead bread. . . . Since I am unable to leave here even for a moment, I am naming [José] Sixto Verduzco, *cura* of Tuzantla, as my representative in the junta." Morelos closed his letter with an admonition: "It would be inadvisable to have more than three members in the junta because it is not easy to develop a republic with the rule of many."⁹

With this endorsement of his plan, Rayón, on August 19, called a meeting of the inhabitants and landowners of the Zitácuaro area, who voted in assembly to authorize the establishment of a junta of three members, to be increased to five if circumstances required. The assembly then decided that Rayón and a group of his associates, including José María Liceaga, José Sixto Verduzco, six high-ranking officers, and four prominent officials, were to select the members and install the junta. To the surprise of no one, Rayón, Liceaga, and Verduzco received the greatest number of votes and were therefore declared elected. Other insurgents received as many as four votes, and even Morelos received one. Rayón obviously dominated all the proceedings at Zitácuaro, and the formalities which he and his associates resorted to were largely in the nature of window dressing to give the election an aspect of legality. With the taking of an oath by the members to defend king and church, the new insurgent government, which was called the Supreme National Junta, was formally installed. Rayón assumed the title of "President of the Supreme Junta and Universal Minister of the Nation."¹⁰

Although Rayón's associates enthusiastically received the junta, many other insurgent leaders, including Morelos, objected to it. Some refused to recognize its authority; others simply ignored it. Morelos thought the titles that Rayón assumed were ridiculous imitations of those in the peninsula, but his main objection to the junta was the allegiance it paid to Ferdinand VII.¹¹ To this charge, Rayón and his colleagues promptly countered that for reasons of expediency — to win Europeans, creoles, and

any others who might be reluctant to rebel against the king —
the decision had been made to use his name. "Our plans are
those of independence," declared the junta in a letter which
since has become one of the best known of the independence
period, "but we insist that the use of the name of Ferdinand VII
will do us no harm."[12] Morelos thereupon agreed to give the
junta his support, though rejecting Rayón's offer to serve as a
fourth member. Moreover, on hearing that Calleja was preparing to attack Zitácuaro, Morelos declared that he was determined to risk his life to uphold the authority and existence
of the Supreme Junta, and that "the security of the three persons
who composed the junta was of the greatest importance, inasmuch as their destruction was the enemy's major objective."[13]
Morelos might not be in agreement with the junta's principles,
nor even on very cordial terms with its members, but so long
as it was the target of Félix María Calleja, he was willing to
support it.

About the middle of November, 1811, Morelos began what
has usually been called his second campaign. He hoped ultimately to take Mexico City and Puebla, but his immediate
objectives were to extend the revolution in the area north of
the capital and to distract enemy forces threatening Zitácuaro.
In late November after Morelos took Tlapa, he received a report
that the viceroy was as frightened as a "scared rooster," and
was contemplating leaving the capital for Vera Cruz.[14] At
Chiutla the insurgents engaged a royalist force commanded
by Mateo Muzitu, whose hatred of Morelos was so intense that
he had cast a special cannon which he named "Mata Morelos."[15]
The insurgents took the town by storm, and although the captured Muzitu offered 50,000 pesos to spare his life, he was shot,
together with the other Spaniards captured. This execution has
led to charges of extreme and needless cruelty on Morelos' part,
but it should be remembered that in guerrilla-type operations,
neither faction gave any quarter whatever, nor expected it.
The inevitable fate of the principal prisoners taken by both

sides was the firing squad; lesser prisoners were confined in a camp near Zacatula where the heat and heavy labor made death just as inevitable but more gradual.

At Chiutla, Morelos divided his forces into three parts: the first, under Miguel Bravo, was to march to the south against Ometepec and occupy the surrounding country; the second, under Galeana, was to attack Taxco to the west; while the third, commanded by Morelos himself, was to move northward, take Izúcar and open the way to Puebla. Taxco and Izúcar soon fell to the insurgents, and Morelos wrote a subordinate that he was preparing to enter Cuautla de las Amilpas where he would formulate plans for attacking the supply lines between Vera Cruz and the capital.[16]

Cuautla fell to the insurgents on Christmas day, and although the way to Puebla seemed open, Morelos suddenly turned to the west to join Galeana in Taxco. What was the reason for this move, in view of the almost incalculable advantage the control of such a vital center as Puebla would afford? Morelos later said that he turned the other way because he was worried about a royalist force at Toluca commanded by Rosendo Porlier and the possibility that it might descend on Taxco and recapture the entire area to the south.[17] Whether Morelos' move to the west was to provide at least indirect assistance to the Junta of Zitácuaro, as Bustamante claims, or whether it was simply to confirm insurgent control over the Taxco-Tenango area, as Alamán states, is not very important;[18] but there is at least one Mexican historian who, after a careful study of the strategic possibilities, thinks that Morelos' failure to move in the direction of Puebla at that time constituted one of his greatest military blunders.[19]

On January 1, 1812, the day that Morelos entered Taxco, Calleja appeared before Zitácuaro. Apparently the members of the junta were confident that the royalist assault could be successfully resisted. Liceaga wrote that the enemy forces numbered six thousand men, and that their commanders considered the destruction of Zitácuaro "as the most important task which has confronted them since the beginning of the insurrection." But he added, optimistically, "that we will lose only if God wishes to punish us, because the local situation — our arms, supplies, and the high morale of the people — should give us the victory."[20] If Liceaga meant what he said, he was fooling himself; but perhaps he was only trying to bolster his own flagging spirits.

Calleja made elaborate plans for attack, and when all was ready, his forces surrounded the town and began to surge forward from all directions simultaneously, their superior gunnery enabling them to advance almost at will. Zitácuaro was doomed.[21] Somehow, the junta members effected their escape, and after many difficulties made their way successfully to Tlalchapa and then to Sultepec, which became the new seat for Rayón's insurgent government. The battle of Zitácuaro was a deadly blow for the insurgent cause, and more particularly for Rayón's power and prestige. His officers began to assert their independence, and Rayón found himself no longer able to command the respect of those who formerly had supported him. He wrote that he had become disgusted with his associates and their "childish dispositions and weak characters."[22] The 19th-century Mexican historian and statesman José María Luis Mora speculates that if the defenders of Zitácuaro, who enjoyed a situation a thousand times more advantageous than Morelos' forces at Cuautla a short time later, had been able to resist for a month or two, Morelos could have become master of Puebla and perhaps the capital itself.[23] Although the comment may be a bit extreme, it nevertheless is worthy of note.

During the month of January, Morelos and his forces, after driving Porlier back to Toluca, retired eastward by way of Cuernavaca to Cuautla, arriving at the latter town on February 9, 1812.[24] Preparations were immediately renewed for the attack on Puebla. Morelos' army, which numbered about three thousand men, including well-trained divisions under the command

of Leonardo Bravo, Hermenegildo Galeana, and Mariano Matamoros, constituted a new and far more formidable menace to
the viceregal power than the Junta of Zitácuaro. Once again
the Mexican capital became a center of turmoil and confusion,
and once again a panic-stricken viceroy called upon his ever-
dependable commander, Calleja, to smash the grave new threat
only some fifty miles to the south. Here, in a letter to Calleja,
is the way the viceroy described the situation:

The capital of Mexico has been encircled by gangs of bandits, who
have interrupted communications, mail facilities, and supply lines
from all directions. . . . The occupation of Querétaro has obstructed
trade with the interior, and it is absolutely impossible to ship quick-
silver and gunpowder, and the other products of the mines which
are so indispensable to our manufacturing processes. The most dis-
tressing privation has resulted in the provinces of Guanajuato, San
Luis Potosí, Zacatecas, Nueva Galicia, and others in the interior. . . .
The towns in the vicinity of Valladolid interrupt communications
and trade from that city to this. . . . Worse still is the road from Puebla.
The rebels in considerable force have occupied many towns and
haciendas in that province; they have destroyed everything, and
have insulted the unfortunate residents . . . to such an extent that
they live in a state of constant anxiety. . . . This same sort of turmoil
has caused the greatest difficulty in communicating with Oaxaca and
its province; and the same is true of Vera Cruz. . . .

All these evils — the danger of our commerce with Acapulco being
interrupted, the impossibility of carrying an overseas trade, the difficulty of shipping goods to the interior, the deprivation of a million
pesos which the treasury should have received from a certain ship-
ment, the imminence of the collapse of the port of Vera Cruz to the
insurgent forces — all these factors are caused by the person of
Morelos, the chief leader of the insurrection, of which he is the
guiding genius. . . .

It is then essential to conceive a plan to strike Morelos and his
band a smashing blow that will terrorize his followers to such a
degree that they will at least desert him, even if they do not seize him.

Their principal occupied points are Izúcar, Cuautla, and Taxco. . . .
The plan is to make a simultaneous attack on Izúcar and Cuautla.
The operation would be more complete with an attack on Taxco
also, but it is undesirable in that it would require further subdivision

of forces, and there is not a sufficient number in Toluca for this undertaking.[25]

Accordingly, the viceroy ordered Calleja and his Army of the Center, reinforced by a division from Puebla, to attack Cuautla and then to return to the capital after Morelos had been dealt a crushing blow. Meanwhile, Morelos, having been advised of Calleja's advance, sent out a call to the junta at Sultepec and to all the troops under his command, including those at Izúcar, Chiautla, Ometepec, Chilpancingo, and Acapulco, to send all the help possible.[26] The stage was now set at Cuautla for the showdown between the royalist forces of Calleja and the insurgents under Morelos. All Mexico awaited the outcome. "With the fate of Cuautla," wrote Calleja to the viceroy, "will be decided the fate of this kingdom."[27]

REFERENCES

1. Hugh M. Hamill, "Early Psychological Warfare in the Hidalgo Revolt," p. 212.
2. Hidalgo to Morelos, Celaya, November 12, 1810, manuscript in San Jacinto Museum of History. I have photostatic copy.
3. Caruso, *The Liberators of Mexico*, p. 66.
4. Bancroft, *History of Mexico*, IV, 255.
5. *Ibid.*, p. 275.
6. *Apuntes para la biografía del Exmo. Sr. Lic. D. Ignacio López Rayón*, p. 1. This is a biographical sketch by Rayón's son, written as an introduction to his father's diary, which covers his activities from August 1, 1812 to September 7, 1814.
7. Ignacio Rayón and José María Liceaga to Félix Calleja, Zacatecas, April 22, 1811, Hernández y Dávalos (ed.), *Colección*, III, 279-80.
8. *Idem* to *idem*, *ibid.*
9. Morelos to Rayón, Tixtla, August 13, 1811, *Morelos documentos*, I, 126-27.
10. Alamán, *Historia de México*, II, 380; see also Hernández y Dávalos (ed.), *Colección*, III, 403.
11. Alamán, in his *Historia de México*, II, 380, says that Morelos later declared during his trial that "there was no reason for deceiving the people by doing one thing while pretending something else — that is to say, to fight for independence while supposing that it could be accomplished through Ferdinand VII." I have never been able to find this statement in the testimony given by Morelos at his trial.
12. The Supreme National Junta to Morelos, Zitácuaro, September 4, 1811, Hernández y Dávalos (ed.), *Colección*, I, 874. This document was captured from Morelos at Cuautla.
13. Morelos to Rayón, El Veladero, October 23, 1811, *ibid.*, III, 405.
14. *Idem* to *idem*, Tlapa, November 22, 1811, *ibid.*, 446.
15. Bustamante, *Cuadro histórico*, II, 24.

16. Morelos to Esteván Pérez, (Izúcar ?) (December, 1811 ?), *Morelos documentos*, I, 27.

17. Testimony of Morelos, *ibid.*, II, 340.

18. Bustamante, *Cuadro histórico*, II, 29; Alamán, *Historia de México*, II, 464, note 23.

19. Antonio Peñafiel, *Ciudades coloniales y capitales de la Republica Mexicana*, p. 79.

20. Liceaga to Morelos, Zitácuaro, December 18, 1811, Archivo General de la Nación, Operaciones de Guerra, Morelos, tomo V.

21. For military details, see documents in *Morelos documentos*, I, 31-46; H. G. Ward, in his *Mexico in 1827* (p. 189), says that Zitácuaro was still in ruins when he saw it in 1826.

22. Rayón to Morelos, Tlalchapa, January 18, 1812, in Alamán, *Historia de México*, II, 444.

23. José María Luís Mora, *México y sus revoluciones*, IV, 312.

24. Testimony of Morelos, *Morelos documentos*, II, 341.

25. Venegas to Calleja, Mexico City, February 8, 1812, in Carlos Bustamante, *Campañas del General D. Félix María Calleja*, pp. 159-65.

26. Luís Chavez Orozco, *El sitio de Cuautla*, p. 35.

27. Calleja to Venegas, Campo sobre Cuautla, March 12, 1812, *Morelos documentos*, I, 310.

CHAPTER VI

THE CONQUEST OF
THE SOUTH

CUAUTLA de las Amilpas was highly suitable for defense, since it was situated on a rolling plain and surrounded by thick groves of trees growing close to the buildings. The main street ran north and south for about half a league and connected the convents of San Diego and Santo Domingo. A thick wall protected the greater part of the west side of the town, while on the east there flowed a broad, swift river. The insurgents applied themselves with great energy to prepare for the coming attack, fortifying the plazas and convents and digging an elaborate network of trenches to link the main defenses. "Cuautla is fortified with intelligence," reported Calleja, after he had made an initial test of its system of defenses.[1] The best estimate of the number of troops who served with the insurgents is between 4,000 and 4,500, while the royalists had twice that figure after they received reinforcements early in March. But strength in armament was about evenly matched, each side employing from twenty to twenty-five artillery pieces and cannon of various calibers.[2]

The main attack began on the morning of February 19. The royalists advanced in four columns, but so effective was the insurgent fire, which repulsed charge after charge, that Calleja was forced to withdraw his men in the afternoon after suffering heavy losses. Plans of the royalists had to be revised, and a council of war that night decided that a siege must be laid. "Cuautla is defended with 12,000 men, 2,500 guns, and 30 cannon," reported Calleja with deliberate exaggeration. Great losses would be sustained, he said, and a siege had become necessary, requiring more men, artillery, military stores, ammunition, and time. But Calleja expressed confidence that if the siege could be applied effectively, Morelos could be smashed in six or eight days.[3]

The royalists began a vigorous bombardment on March 10, with Calleja pounding from the west, and Ciriaco de Llano, who had arrived with reinforcements, from the east. The inhabitants of the town, frightened at first by the downpour of shot and shell, quickly became accustomed to it; and the children found they could earn a few reales for gathering the cannon balls that fell into the streets.[4] But four days of intensive bombardment brought no appreciable change, and an attempt by the royalists to divert the flow of the river to cut the town's water supply also failed. The morale of the insurgents was still high; communications with the outside were still intact, and Morelos and his leaders still as determined and confident as ever. Morelos took the occasion to taunt his adversary with the following note, written in the middle of the siege:

He who dies for the true religion and for his country, does not die unhappily but gloriously. You, who wish to die for the cause of Napoleon, will end in the same way that is designed for the others. You are not the one who determines the final moment of this army, but rather it is God, who has decided the punishment of the Europeans, and who has declared that the Americans should recover their rights. I am a Catholic, and for that reason, I say to you that you should return to your native country, because in accordance with the circumstances of the war, [victory] will be ours on the day that God decrees. Aside from this, you do not have to worry, because even though this army should be defeated, there still remains all America, which knows its rights and which is determined to destroy all *gachupines*. You no doubt believe that king D. Sebastian will appear on his white horse to help you win the war, but the Americans know better; no longer are you able to deceive them with your false proclamations. I suppose that it will be necessary for an army with trousers to come to help Señor Calleja destroy this courageous division, for the petticoat army he has now has not been able even to enter the outskirts of this town. If the occasion should arise, while I am working in my office, have your army fire some shells at me, because I am lonesome without them.[5]

Meanwhile, within the town the food supply had steadily deteriorated. From captured insurgents Calleja learned that during the month of March the insurgents had an ample supply of bread, corn, beans, and water, though there was a shortage of meat, while by the middle of April, the only sustenance left was corn. Henry G. Ward, who later was British Minister to Mexico, wrote that during the siege "a cat sold for six pesos, a lizard for two, and rats for a peso apiece."[6] An insurgent prisoner told the royalists that the defenders ate tortillas in the morning, tortillas at noon, and tortillas at night, and that there were from twenty-five to thirty persons dying daily during the last part of April.[7] At one time there were more than three hundred cases of malnutrition in the Hospital de San Diego alone, and the suffering became more intense each day. Calleja could not hide his admiration, declaring that "their fanaticism compensates for their lack of food." He later added: "If the devotion and activity of the defenders of Cuautla were in behalf of morality and directed to a just cause, they would merit some day a distinguished place in history. . . . This priest is a second Mohammed."[8]

On the other hand the royalists were having their troubles. Calleja complained about the disagreeable climate which had caused the spread of dysentery and endemic fever among the troops; fatigue had gripped the army; the early rains had made a swamp out of his camp site, and had rendered his artillery all but useless; the troops had not been paid because there was a shortage of funds; morale, therefore, was low; and his own health had deteriorated steadily.[9] So it must have been gratifying to the royalists to receive news that the viceroy had published, on April 1, a general amnesty which had been issued by the Spanish Cortes on the previous November 9, 1811, granting a pardon to those insurgents who would renounce the revolution, lay down their arms, and acknowledge the authority of the viceregal government.[10]

Published by Calleja on April 17, this proclamation was received by the hard-pressed defenders with great joy. Although there must have been great pressure on Morelos to accept the offer, he considered it a ruse, and rejected it completely. Bustamante says that when Morelos received a copy of the edict, he replied sharply that he was extending equal mercy to Calleja and the other Spaniards.[11]

Nevertheless, the insurgent position was becoming increasingly untenable. After an attempt to obtain help from Rayón had failed, Morelos decided that the only course left was evacuation. He ordered that preparations be made in great detail. According to plan, the soldiers and the people were mustered in the plaza of San Diego just before midnight of May 1, and at two in the morning the march from the town began. Galeana, commanding a thousand infantrymen, led the advance guard. The Bravos and Morelos led two hundred fifty cavalrymen, a corps of troops armed with slings and lances, and the main body of the townspeople; and a Captain Anzures brought up the rear-guard infantry and artillery.[12] The insurgent columns left by the north entrance, cut down the royalist guard posted just outside the gate, and proceeded eastward in such silence that even after they had been on the march for two hours, their movements had escaped detection. Ironically, at that very moment Calleja was writing the viceroy that he was planning to evacuate the place, since his health had deteriorated so greatly.[13]

Not until the insurgent band had crossed the river did the royalists discover what had happened. But in a flash, Llano's cavalry was on the insurgent flank, and Calleja's force was approaching. A fierce battle was fought which lasted more than an hour. Resistance against such overwhelming odds became hopeless; Morelos therefore gave the order to disperse and to rendezvous in Izúcar.[14] The confusion which followed was indescribable: royalists fired on each other; insurgents and defenseless townspeople were cut down by the hundreds; and for a distance of seven leagues the royalists pursued the fleeing insurgents, with the result that the roads were so covered with cadavers that one could hardly take a step without falling on them.[15] Many lost their way, and families became separated. "Even today," wrote a contemporary in 1826 who had witnessed the event, "there are men and women who are separated from their respective wives and husbands, and who do not know whether or not they are alive."[16] Morelos, who broke two ribs when his horse fell into a ditch, fled in the direction of Zacatepec with an escort of about seventy men. The royalists followed in hot pursuit. Practically the entire escort of Morelos was sacrificed to permit the escape of their chief, who, almost alone, finally reached Izúcar and Chiautla.[17]

The most reasoned guess as to the number of insurgents lost is about three thousand, or a thousand less than Calleja reported.[18] A great percentage of the number were unarmed residents of Cuautla rather than troops. Also lost were Morelos' private archive and almost all the insurgent armament, plus considerable territory which the royalists recaptured while the siege was in progress. The greatest loss, however, was the capture of Leonardo Bravo, who was offered his release if he would prevail upon his brothers and his son to abandon the revolution. Leonardo declined the offer and he was executed on September 13.[19]

On the other hand, Morelos had not been captured, nor had his army been entirely crushed, although the royalists had spent almost two million pesos in the effort. The viceroy claimed a great victory, but when Calleja returned to the capital on May 16, his reception was far less enthusiastic than that following Zitácuaro. Ward writes that in a comedy which was presented in Mexico City several nights afterward, a soldier was introduced, who on returning from battle gave his general a turban and boasted, "Here is the turban of the Moor, whom I took prisoner." "And the Moor himself?" inquired the general. "Oh, he unfortunately escaped!" Whereupon the audience roared with laughter.[20]

Thus ended the 72-day siege of Cuautla, a titanic struggle between the forces of the old order and the new — a struggle which Mexican writers have described as one of the most glorious in the annals of military history. To be sure, Cuautla does not have the historical significance of engagements such as the Alamo, or Verdun, or Corregidor, but like them, it is the embodiment of a courageous and spirited resistance against a relentless and overpowering foe. Historically, Cuautla may be viewed without exaggeration as one of Morelos' most inspired achievements, for he had prevented Calleja from bringing the revolution to a close in 1812. Since Morelos had escaped and continued to remain at large, Viceroy Venegas was forced to announce, with some embarrassment, that the reward which he had been offering for Morelos' capture was still in effect, for he was as determined as ever, he said, "to liberate the world from one of its most hideous monsters."[21]

The insurgents accomplished little in the six months' period following the evacuation of Cuautla, until Morelos took Oaxaca. Most of their military operations were confined to the Tehuacán-Orizaba area, but they never developed an over-all strategy, and their net gains in the area for the rest of the year remained negligible. They recovered several towns south of Cuautla, such as Chilapa, which the insurgents had given up during the siege, only to lose them again when they moved on to another area. Late in July, Morelos was forced to make a diversionary move to the east to rescue a beleaguered insurgent force commanded by Valerio Trujano at Huajuapán, which had been under siege for more than three months. Morelos won a great victory in lifting the siege, and although the way seemed open to Oaxaca, he preferred to move northward instead, arriving at Tehuacán de las Granadas on August 10, where he remained about two months.[22]

Early in October, Morelos ordered the valiant Trujano to move in the direction of Puebla. Establishing headquarters at Rancho de la Virgen, about halfway between Tehuacán and Puebla, Trujano was attacked by a royalist force under Saturnino Samaniego. Trujano fell in battle. A rout would have been certain had it not been for the arrival of Galeana, who rallied the insurgents, drove the royalists from the field, and carried the body of the fallen hero to Tehuacán, where Morelos ordered it buried with military honors.[23]

Morelos himself took the field about the middle of October, setting out to the northwest. He explained to Rayón that he was still thinking of the conquest of Puebla and Vera Cruz, but that his immediate objective was to secure possession of one hundred silver bars which the junta had promised him but which had never been delivered.[24] At Ozumba, to the west of Puebla, Morelos recovered the silver, and learned of the proximity of a royalist convoy carrying provisions and ammunition to be used to besiege him in Tehuacán. He also discovered that the royalists had drawn so heavily on the manpower of the area that Orizaba had been left unprotected. After a hasty and unsuccessful attack on the convoy, Morelos marched with all possible speed, attacked Orizaba on October 29, and took it within two hours' time.[25] He captured a vast quantity of booty, including cannon, government tobacco, and currency. Morelos distributed some of the tobacco to his soldiers, some to the farmers in the area, and set the rest on fire, boasting that its destruction would deprive the viceroy of funds sufficient to wage war for seven years.[26] The claim proved to be exaggerated, however, for it was later revealed that the royalists had succeeded in hiding vast quantities of tobacco which the insurgents had failed to find.[27] Leaving Orizaba on October 31 to return to Tehuacán, Morelos and his forces were intercepted and dispersed on the way, but he was able nevertheless to collect his scattered units and make preparations for extending the revolution to the southward.

Thus far in 1812 the insurgents had little to show for their efforts, and the cause of independence was in desperate need of a military victory. Perhaps, as Carlos Bustamante has suggested, it would have been far more advantageous to the insurgents to have made a vigorous and determined effort to attack and dis-

THE SOLDIER

rupt the royalist supply lines from Mexico City to Vera Cruz.[28] Guerrilla-type operations, involving destructive hit-and-run tactics and avoiding formal open military engagements, could have done irreparable damage to the viceregal government. Morelos, however, greatly desired a quick, decisive victory; and dubious about the possibilities of obtaining one in the Puebla-Vera Cruz theatre, he fixed his sights on the provincial capital city of Oaxaca.

Morelos remained in Tehuacán only seven days, making preparations for the expedition to Oaxaca in the greatest secrecy.[29] He called in the men under Victor Bravo in the Mixteca, and those serving in Izúcar under Matamoros, who was named second-in-command of Morelos' army. An insurgent force of some five thousand men, well-trained, adequately supplied, and ably led by such veterans as Galeana, the Bravos, and Matamoros, began the march toward Oaxaca on November 10. After two weeks Morelos' army was on the outskirts of Oaxaca demanding that the royalist garrison surrender. Meanwhile, the viceroy's forces had re-occupied Tehuacán and Orizaba soon after the insurgents left.

An implacable enemy of Morelos and one of the most outspoken foes of the revolution was Antonio Bergosa y Jordán, Bishop of Oaxaca, who was nominated Archbishop of Mexico by the Cádiz regency in 1811 to succeed Lizana y Beaumont. Because of unsettled conditions in Oaxaca at that time, however, several prominent citizens of that capital persuaded Bergosa to remain in his diocese and use his influence against the revolution until the situation became more stabilized there.[30] Not only did Bergosa begin to launch a deadly volley of bans, excommunications, censures, and fulminations against the rebel priests, but he also raised and equipped a body of ecclesiastics to resist any threat to the Oaxaca area by force. Morelos he described as a man with "horns and a tail."[31] But like the other rebel priests, Morelos ignored the censures because he believed them to be invalid.

We have heard with sadness and regret the censures of the Oaxaca chapter [he said] but our consciences will remain clear and quiet so long as the defenders and adulators of Spain do not prove that the Mexican insurrection is unjust. Upon the truth or falsity of that proposition depends the validity or nullity of the censures imposed by our bishops. If the insurrection is just, we are not obligated to swear our fidelity to Spain, and when the law does not obligate us to do so, censure cannot be brought against the violators of that law. If the law is void, all the effect of the censure is removed, because there is no obligation, contumacy, nor disobedience; neither is there guilt in its transgression. . . . When an American goes over to the Spanish party, he is no longer a heretic; he can receive the sacraments, and the effects of the censure are thereby suspended.[32]

As Morelos approached Oaxaca, he explained to Bishop Bergosa that he came with an "olive branch in one hand and a sword in the other," that the revolution was essentially an effort to break the chains of a slavery that had lasted for three centuries, and that should the demands of the insurgents be met, the bishop and all the clergy in the diocese would be preserved, together with their immunities and benefits.[33] But Bergosa rejected the offer. As the insurgents entered the city, he fled first to Vera Cruz and then to Mexico City in the following March to continue his relentless attacks on the rebel priests.[34]

The insurgents swept into the city of Oaxaca on November 25.[35] So great was the temptation for loot, so starved were the insurgent forces for victory, and so intent on revenge were they as a result of the diatribes and insults heaped upon them by the Spanish civil and ecclesiastical leaders in Oaxaca, that Morelos was unable to restrain them, with the result that the city was completely sacked. Insurgent prisoners found by Morelos were freed, placed on horseback, and paraded around the square to impress the townspeople with the barbarity of which the royalists were capable. The royalist commanders were executed, but the ecclesiastics were spared. When Jacinto Moreno, Morelos' former instructor of Latin grammar, interceded in behalf of some two hundred prisoners, he was able to obtain the release of all but thirty whom Morelos especially distrusted.[36]

Morelos' brilliant victory at Oaxaca greatly bolstered the fortune of the insurgents, enhanced his own personal prestige, and brought a vast amount of material benefits. "This beautiful province is worthy of your attention," wrote Morelos to Rayón, "for it will serve as a basis for the conquest of the whole kingdom; it is the first capital which we have taken which has a unity of its own; it can be defended with only a few men; and it has resources in men, mines, tobacco, ports, and cochineal, all of which can be used as effective weapons."[37] Moreover, the forces of Morelos confiscated a considerable quantity of jewels, silver, personal effects, and grain, as well as the sum of three million pesos, according to the estimate of one Oaxaca resident.[38] For the time being at least, much of the uncertainty which from the beginning had plagued the insurgents respecting their financial affairs in conducting the revolution was removed.

For almost two and a half months Oaxaca was Morelos' headquarters. During that time Morelos brought the surrounding countryside under effective control, organized and trained new divisions of militia, increased the pay of the soldiers, improved their equipment, and established an armory, which he placed under the direction of Manuel Mier y Terán, who had joined the insurgent forces preceding the attack on Oaxaca.[39] Administrative reforms included the appointment of José María Murguía as intendant of the province of Oaxaca, and the establishment of a *ayuntamiento* for the city under the leadership of the creoles. Morelos issued regulations regarding the hours to be maintained by business houses, the carrying of firearms, observance of the curfew, and the use of a badge for personal identification. Lastly, a Junta of Protection and Public Confidence was created to maintain public order and security. With the completion of the work of reform, a great ceremony was held, in which all took a solemn oath to the Supreme Junta. Morelos appeared in a splendid new uniform, a gift of Mariano Matamoros. Magnificently embroidered in gold, and carrying the insignia of the rank of captain-general, it symbolized Morelos at the peak of his military career, acknowledged by friends and foes alike as the first chief of the revolution.[40]

Early in 1813 Morelos began to make preparations for a campaign against the port of Acapulco. Not only did he desire to fulfill the commission of Hidalgo which he had failed to complete in 1810, but he also felt the need of a seaport that would improve commercial relations with foreign powers, and the possession of which at the same time would deprive the viceroy's government of vital imports. A number of authorities have severely criticized the decision of Morelos to take Acapulco. They have argued convincingly that its conquest was obviously time-consuming and expensive, but productive of only limited gains at best. Why waste time, money, and manpower on a fortress which was virtually impregnable, it has been asked, when the same results could have been achieved through a determined assault on the supply and communication lines of the royalists lying between the port and the capital? Aguirre Colorado, who has made the most thorough investigation of Morelos' Acapulco operations, puts it as follows:

Instead of attacking Puebla or surprising the weak garrisons of Córdoba and Orizaba, or of attempting a crushing moral and economic blow at the viceregal government; instead of devoting himself chiefly to crushing the disorganized royalist troops being used basically for protecting convoys . . .; instead of adopting a plan along any of those lines, especially the last-mentioned one, which would have brought decisive results, he chose to drive on Acapulco.[41]

The Guadalupe society, secret partisans of independence in Mexico City, and the insurgents' chief source of information about viceregal affairs, insisted, rightly or wrongly, that the opportunity was ripe for Morelos to advance toward the capital — that the whole metropolitan population would rise up as a unit on hearing of the approach of his army. Morelos, however, chose to ignore their pleadings, and set out with an army of three thousand for Acapulco on February 9, 1813, leaving a garrison to defend Oaxaca. "Acapulco," wrote Morelos to one of his lieutenants, "is a port which the insurgent cause should acquire and keep; Vera Cruz is next in importance, and although San Blas is third, it could be ignored if we could take the first two."[42] The itinerary passed through San Pablo Huizo and Yanhuitlán to the northwest; it then swung abruptly to the southwest to Ometepec, and from there it moved along the southern coast to Quetzala and Cruz Grande. The main body of the army arrived on the outskirts of Acapulco late in March. Matamoros, Galeana, the Bravos, and Guerrero were left at various points along the way to complete the subjugation of the southern coastal region.[43]

It will be remembered that Acapulco was situated on the west side of the harbor, and that on the east side stood the castle fortress which served, together with two small forts, as the city's main defense. The port was ably commanded at that time by Pedro Antonio Vélez, a creole from Córdoba, who had a smaller force but heavier guns than the insurgents. Moreover, he had control of the sea and the use of two brigantines, *San Carlos* and *Guadalupita*.

The insurgents began their main attack on April 6, after their customary ultimatum to surrender had been rejected.[44] Within a week they had surrounded the city from the land side, and by the middle of the month it was in their hands. Morelos then directed his attention to the castle, the last remaining stronghold of royalist power in southern Mexico. A siege was laid, but progress was slow because of the lack of heavy artillery. Moreover, the insurgents were unable to check the flow of supplies to the fortress from Roqueta Island, situated near the mouth of the harbor. Accordingly, on the night of June 9, Pedro Galeana, nephew of the great insurgent commander, and Isidoro Montes de Oca, landed eighty men in a surprise move that not only captured the island but the *Guadalupita* as well. The insurgents were thus able to tighten the blockade considerably, even if they could not completely close it.[45]

As the summer months of 1813 wore on, the siege of Acapulco

became increasingly a sordid story of heat and hardship, suffering and disease. Morelos in mid-August decided to strike. Discarding the suggestion to set fire to the fortress, for fear of taking the lives of the women, children, the aged, and the feeble, he ordered on the night of August 17 that the castle be surrounded and stormed. The insurgents kept up a heavy fire all night and by dawn were preparing to scale the walls. The attack made further resistance futile, and Vélez agreed to an armistice, which was drawn up and signed on August 19. Morelos' terms were lenient. Spaniards were given passports to any place they pleased, so long as they did not join the royalists, while the native-born men were mustered into Morelos' army. The next day an insurgent flag waved above the fortress castle of San Diego de Acapulco, and the commission which Morelos had received from Hidalgo had at last been fulfilled.[46]

The conquest of Acapulco meant that Morelos was master of an expanse of territory stretching from Guatemala on the east to Colima on the west, and from the Pacific Ocean on the south to a line roughly approximating the nineteenth parallel of latitude. The area included the greater portion of the modern states of Oaxaca and Guerrero, and the southern part of the states of Vera Cruz, Puebla, Mexico, and Michoacán.

Morelos' success as a military commander, in spite of his complete lack of formal military training, was achieved largely because of his superb knowledge of terrain and topography, his inherent administrative and organizational ability, judgment of men and choice of officer material, close attention to the minutest detail, strict training and disciplinary requirements, and his strong emphasis on surprise, deception, and mobility. Mexican historians have gone overboard in singing their praises of Morelos as a military genius. He would probably be the first to deny this claim. Although it has been said that he won twenty-five out of thirty-six engagements, it should be pointed out that he lost many important ones, that his strategy was often defective and short-sighted, and that he committed a number of costly blunders, as practically every Mexican historian will admit.

Time was to reveal that Acapulco was one of those blunders. Strategically, the circumventing of the port would have accomplished as much as its capture. The seven months that Morelos spent in such useless and wasteful military operations gave Calleja the best part of the year to carry out his plans to destroy the revolutionary chiefs in the north, and then to turn his united strength upon those in the south. The conquest of Acapulco, while seemingly representing Morelos' military fortunes at their height, in actuality marked the beginning of their decline.

From Acapulco, Morelos left in haste for Chilpancingo to formulate plans for the new insurgent government. Before that move may be discussed, however, it is necessary to turn to the important developments which had been taking place in the capital while Morelos was conquering the south.

REFERENCES

1. Calleja to Venegas, Campo de Quautlisco, February 19, 1812, *Morelos documentos*, I, 292.
2. Nicolás Rangel, *José María Morelos*, pp. 15-16.
3. Calleja to Venegas, Campo sobre Cuautla, February 20, 1812, *Morelos documentos*, I, 297.
4. H. G. Ward, *Mexico in 1827*, I, 194.
5. Morelos to Calleja, (Cuautla ?), (March-April, 1812 ?), *Morelos documentos*, I, 326-27.
6. H. G. Ward, *Mexico in 1827*, I, 196.
7. Testimony of José Durán de Huerta, Campo de Cuautla, April 18, 1812, *Morelos documentos*, I, 348.
8. Calleja to Venegas, Campo sobre Cuautla, April 5, 1812, *ibid.*, p. 328.
9. *Idem* to *idem*, April 24, 1812, *ibid.*, pp. 357-58.
10. Proclamation of Calleja, Campo sobre Cuautla, April 17, 1812, *ibid.*, 343-44.
11. Bustamante, *Cuadro histórico*, II, 71.
12. Calleja to Venegas, Cuautla, May 4, 1812, *Morelos documentos*, I, 368.
13. *Idem* to *idem*, Cuautla, May 2, 1812, *ibid.*, I, 367.
14. Bustamante, *Cuadro histórico*, II, 72.
15. Calleja to Venegas, Cuautla, May 4, 1812, *Morelos documentos*, I, 369.
16. Edmundo O'Gorman (ed.), "El Sitio de Cuautla," *Boletín del Archivo General de la Nación*, IX (1938), 455.
17. Calleja to Venegas, Cuautla, May 4, 1812, *Morelos documentos*, I, 369.
18. Edmundo O'Gorman (ed.), "El Sitio de Cuautla," p. 453.
19. Luís Chavez Orozco, *El sitio de Cuautla*, pp. 187-88.
20. H. G. Ward, *Mexico in 1827*, I, 200.

21. Proclamation of Venegas, May 11, 1812, Hernández y Dávalos (ed.), *Colección*, IV, 166.

22. Testimony of Morelos, *Morelos documentos*, II, 344.

23. *Ibid.;* Bancroft, *History of Mexico*, IV, 477, note 12.

24. Testimony of Morelos, *Morelos documentos*, II, 344.

25. *Ibid.*, p. 345; Morelos to José Antonio Andrade, October 29, 1812, *ibid.*, I, 59-60.

26. Morelos to Rayón, Tehuacán, November 2, 1812, Hernández y Dávalos (ed.), *Colección*, IV, 656.

27. The Guadalupes to Morelos, Mexico City, (March ?) 6, 1813, Morelos Papers, LAC UT. The Guadalupe society, their activities, and their important correspondence with Morelos are discussed in Chapter VIII.

28. Bustamante, *Cuadro histórico*, II, 196.

29. See Morelos to Manuel Sanchez de Cueva, Cuicatlán, November 17, 1812, Emilio del Castillo Negrete, *México en el siglo XIX*, V, 331. This letter, deliberately left in Tehuacán to throw the royalists off the track, stated that Morelos had left for Puebla.

30. Alamán, *Historia de México*, III, 439.

31. Trial of José de San Martín, Hernández y Dávalos (ed.), *Colección*, VI, 409.

32. Quoted in Mariano Cuevas, *Historia de la iglesia en México*, V, 88-89.

33. Morelos to Bishop Antonio Bergosa y Jordán, Campo sobre Oaxaca, November 25, 1812, *Morelos documentos*, I, 163.

34. The Guadalupes to Morelos, Mexico City, July 5, 1813, Morelos Papers, LAC UT.

35. Testimony of Morelos, *Morelos documentos*, II, 346.

36. *Ibid.*, p. 346-47.

37. Morelos to Rayón, Oaxaca, December 16, 1812, Hernández y Dávalos (ed.), *Colección*, IV, 690. A facsimile is given in Julio Zárate, *La guerra de independencia*, p. 330.

38. *Relación* of Doña María Micaela Frontaura, Oaxaca, January 28, 1813, Hernández y Dávalos (ed.), *Colección*, IV, 843.

39. Alamán, *Historia de México*, III, 329.

40. Decree of Morelos, Oaxaca, November 25, 1812, *Morelos documentos*, I, 146; December 19, 1812, *ibid.*, p. 164; Bancroft, *History of Mexico*, IV, 488.

41. Aguirre Colorado, *Campañas de Morelos sobre Acapulco*, p. 93.

42. Morelos to Ignacio Ayala, Yanhuitlán, February 17, 1813, Hernández y Dávalos (ed.), *Colección*, IV, 859. The original is in the Morelos Papers LAC UT.

43. For details see diary of Juan N. Rosains, in Carlos Bustamante, *Suplemento a la historia de los tres siglos de México durante el gobierno español escrita por el Padre Andrés Cavo*.

44. Testimony of Morelos, *Morelos documentos*, II, 348.

45. Bustamante, *Cuadro histórico*, II, 265.

46. The documentary material on the siege and capture of Acapulco has been published in a number of places, notably, *Morelos documentos*, II, 80-156; Hernández y Dávalos (ed.), *Colección*, VI, 114-197; and Aguirre Colorado, *Campañas de Morelos sobre Acapulco*, pp. 179-214. Bustamante, in his *Cuadro Histórico* (II, 305), tells the story that at a dinner given for the officers of both parties after the surrender, Morelos proposed the following toast: "Long live Spain, but Spain as a sister, not as a ruler over America."

CHAPTER VII

EVENTS IN MEXICO CITY

AN important and dramatic, yet largely unfamiliar aspect of the movement for Mexican independence was the part played by a secret organization of insurgent patriots of Mexico City who called themselves the Guadalupes.[1] Although this group contributed to the cause of independence in a variety of ways, their chief service was espionage and the transmission of vital information to the insurgent commanders in the field. Taking copies of the viceroy's correspondence from his secretary's office,[2] they drafted comprehensive reports for their insurgent colleagues covering a multitude of topics: royalist military information and plans, troop and convoy movements, size and location of the viceroy's forces, and recruiting activities; political events in Spain and in Mexico City; governmental finances; status of the revolutionary party in the capital; and developments in connection with the search for foreign assistance. The Guadalupes also helped in the establishment of an insurgent press; smuggled arms, munitions, and supplies; sheltered royalist deserters and fugitive insurgents; and exerted considerable influence in obtaining the election of delegates to the Spanish Cortes in 1812 and 1813 who were sympathetic to Mexican independence.[3]

Although there is some disagreement among authorities as to the time the society originated, probably it came into being soon after the Grito de Dolores. It then took the name "Los Guadalupes" and began to function as a secret organization to assist the independence movement in any way it could. Its membership was drawn largely from the creoles of the professional class in Mexico City and included lawyers, journalists, literary figures, the wives of several of the group, and even some who held responsible positions in the viceroy's government.

There were more than twenty members, of whom Juan Bautista Raz y Guzmán, a lawyer, apparently was the central figure. Many whose names in Mexican history are well known had a connection with the organization, but perhaps were not members: Carlos María Bustamante, Guadalupe Victoria, José Joaquín Fernández de Lizardi, Andrés Quintana Roo, and Leona Vicario, the niece of Raz y Guzmán and, sometime later, the wife of Quintana Roo.[4] Meetings ordinarily were held in the homes of the members, but on occasion they gathered in what appeared to be a week-end social function at the hacienda of León near Mexico City, property of one of the members named Manuel Díaz.[5] The viceregal authorities were extremely concerned about the Guadalupe society and its activities, but until 1814 were unable to compromise its secrecy or reduce its influence in any appreciable way. "A league of rebels, under the name of the Guadalupes, has been growing for more than three years in the heart of this capital," wrote Félix María Calleja after he had become Viceroy of New Spain, and he continued:

it maintains contacts throughout the entire kingdom; it includes within its ranks a great number of well-known people in the government itself; and it directs and encourages the rebel groups in their defeats. From this club the rebels receive as much information as can be conveyed with safety, and accurate accounts of the developments in the capital are forwarded: the status of the forces, munitions, and supplies, all of which is taken from the offices of the government; accounts of the resources of the government, its scarcities and its difficulties; and explanations for the decisions of the viceroy regarding various problems which arise.[6]

Not long after the Guadalupes first established contact with Morelos in September, 1812, political developments in Spain and Mexico City opened new opportunities for them to do effective work for the insurgent cause. It will be remembered that the Junta of Seville had retired to the Isle of León in 1809, where it had turned the government over to a regency of five members. That group, in turn, convoked a national Cortes in September, 1810, which produced, some eighteen months later, the Spanish Constitution of 1812. A typical product of the political liberalism prevailing in the era of the French Revolution, the chief features of the constitution included: popular sovereignty, Catholicism as the established religion, hereditary monarchy, separation of powers, a national legislature based on population, elective municipal offices, freedom of the press, and an administrative chief assisted by an advisory council to govern the provinces.[7] After much hesitation Viceroy Venegas published the constitution on September 28, and a week later, on October 5, proclaimed freedom of the press to be in effect, subject only to a supervisory board of five members, or *junta de censura,* to guard against seditious writings.[8]

Even before the viceroy's proclamation of freedom of the press, however, the Guadalupes had assisted Ignacio Rayón and Morelos in establishing several insurgent publications. From a printer in Mexico City named José Rebelo, the Guadalupes purchased a press for eight hundred pesos and persuaded the printer to work for them in behalf of the insurgent cause. The story is told that the wives of three of the members, escorted by Raz y Guzmán on horseback, smuggled the printing press out of Mexico City. The party arrived at Atizapán, where the press was packed in fruit crates and taken on muleback to Tenango. There it was received by Ignacio Rayón, who immediately sent it to Sultepec, where Rebelo, the printer, and José María Cos, the insurgent editor, established *Ilustrador Americano* in May, 1812.[9] About that time the distinguished writer Andrés Quintana Roo left Mexico City for Sultepec, where he founded *Semanario Patriótico Americano,* printed by the Imprenta de la Nación on the same press that José María Cos received from the Guadalupes. Both papers were published in Sultepec until October, 1812, when they were moved to Tlalpujahua.[10] While this move was under way, the Guadalupes notified Morelos that they had contracted with a printer to help him establish an insurgent publication. Presumably, Morelos used him after the capture of Oaxaca to found *Correo Americano del Sur,* edited at first by José Manuel de Herrera, and later by Carlos María Bustamante.[11]

The new concessions on printing that Viceroy Venegas granted seemed so strange at first that writers scarcely knew what to say. Carlos María Bustamante, in Mexico City at that time, began the first number of his periodical *Juguetillo* with the query: "What can we talk about now?"[12] Soon, however, the capital was flooded with pamphlets highly partisan in tone, produced by writers like Bustamante and José Joaquín Fernández de Lizardi, who did not always bother about having their publications examined by the *junta de censura* before they circulated them. For this reason, the new freedom became such an effective device for propagating revolutionary ideas and undermining the government that Venegas on December 5 suspended the right he had granted only two months before. Some pamphleteers like Lizardi were caught and jailed; others like Bustamante, aided by the Guadalupes, were able to escape. Obviously, the insurgent party denounced the viceroy's action everywhere as "despotism and tyranny at its worst"; and Morelos commented that the granting of the license to print was an example of Spanish duplicity — a deliberate attempt to trap the writers so they could be jailed.[13] The only hope remaining for the insurgent party of Mexico City, wrote the Guadalupes, was to secure the election of members of the *cabildo* who would be sympathetic to the cause and who would therefore demand the complete implementation of the constitution, including freedom of the press.[14]

Another innovation in the Constitution of 1812 was the provision establishing a representative system of government for Spain and the overseas possessions whereby parish electors were to choose *cabildo* members and provincial electors. These in turn were to name the deputies to the Cortes and the provincial deputation. Accordingly, in October, Viceroy Venegas decreed that the choosing of the twenty-five electors to which Mexico City was entitled would take place on November 29, 1812. As a result of the voting held on that day as scheduled, all candidates selected were creoles, not a single European being chosen, nor even anyone favorable to the European party. Overcome with joy, the Guadalupes described the results of the elections as "the first step toward the establishment of Mexican liberty."[15] The viceroy, understandably concerned about the outcome, remained completely silent about holding the other elections. Near the end of December, he finally declared that he had decided to suspend the newly chosen electors, and that he was keeping the old *cabildo* in power until further notice.[16] Thus, as with freedom of the press, the viceroy suspended the second liberal feature of the Constitution of 1812 after it had been in effect for about two months. This setback was no great loss from Morelos' point of view, for nothing less than the complete independence of Mexico would satisfy him from this time on. He no longer had any faith, he said, in the declaration of the Spanish Cortes that Americans were equal to Europeans, for it was lacking in sincerity and had been issued only to betray the native peoples of New Spain.

Only for purposes of deception and flattery [he told the people of Oaxaca in 1812] do the Europeans address us as brothers. If they had proceeded with sincerity and in good faith, they would have declared our independence at the same time that they declared theirs, and they would have given us the liberty of establishing our government, as they have established theirs.[17]

During the latter months of 1812 the Guadalupes were involved in a rather curious episode which began as a plan involving some merchants of Mexico City and then suddenly developed, through the intervention of Viceroy Venegas, as a proposal for a cessation of hostilities. A group of wealthy merchants, owners of a rich cargo which had just been landed at Acapulco, appealed to the Guadalupes in October, 1812, to use their influence to secure from the insurgents permission for the safe passage of the goods to Cuernavaca, where the cargo would be received by government forces and escorted to the capital.

In return for the safe delivery of the cargo the merchants agreed to pay 45,000 pesos, a sum indicative of the advantage the insurgents enjoyed in controlling the territory between Acapulco and the capital. The Guadalupes approved the plan and submitted it to Rayón. Juan Raz y Guzmán was selected to conduct negotiations and work out the details.[18]

Ignacio Rayón viewed the plan with suspicion, but replied that he was making no commitment until he had consulted with Liceaga and Verduzco, his colleagues on the Supreme Junta, and with Morelos. Meanwhile, Rayón learned that the plan involved considerably more than was originally proposed: that the viceroy was desirous of negotiating a cessation of hostilities with the insurgents, details of which were to be arranged in a conference at the hacienda of Tepetongo. There, Juan Bautista Lobo, representing the viceroy, and Tomás Murphi, agent for the merchants, planned to meet Rayón and his associates.[19]

The viceroy's motives respecting the suspension of hostilities are not clear, but probably he was seeking an arrangement in the nature of a truce which would allow him to gain time until the political, financial, and military situation in Mexico City had improved. Rayón wrote Morelos a second time, indicating he would suspend all proceedings if he detected duplicity.[20] On the day agreed upon for the negotiations, however, the viceroy's representative failed to appear, and the whole plan collapsed. The viceroy's motives for suspending negotiations are as difficult to determine as his motives for beginning them in the first place. Negotiations might well have collapsed anyway, since Liceaga and Verduzco had voiced strong objections; and Morelos, who controlled the territory through which the cargo would pass, made his opinion clear that the Spaniards could not be trusted to live up to any agreement, and that the entire matter was an enemy plot to deceive the insurgents.[21]

Particularly alarming to the Guadalupes late in 1812 was the return to a position of authority and influence in viceregal circles of Félix María Calleja. Following his failure to capture

Morelos at Cuautla, Calleja's relations with the viceroy had become so strained that he had surrendered his command of the Army of the Center and had lived in retirement in Mexico City for the remainder of the year. But on December 29, 1812, Viceroy Venegas appointed Calleja military governor of Mexico City, a development the Guadalupes interpreted as a move on the part of the Europeans in Mexico City, who had lost confidence in Venegas, to prepare the way for having Calleja named viceroy. "Should that come about," they wrote, "despotism and tyranny will ascend to the greatest height, for in cruelty, ability, skill, and influence, Calleja surpasses Venegas." Within two months the fears of the Guadalupes were confirmed, for on February 28, 1813, Calleja received orders naming him Viceroy of New Spain.[22]

Félix María Calleja, "the new Tamerlane," as Carlos Bustamante called him,[23] was cold, calculating, efficient, egotistical, and opportunistic. At one time late in 1812 when his relations with Venegas were so strained, Calleja had shown interest in a proposal of the Guadalupes that painted in the most glowing terms the rewards that would be his should he care to join the party of independence. The Guadalupes named two envoys to negotiate with Calleja, and the three fixed a day when he was to join the revolution. But later in a conference which took place the day after Calleja had been named viceroy, the two envoys, not having heard of the appointment, received the shock of their lives as Calleja greeted them: "If you were not my friends, I would have you shot. You are speaking to the Viceroy of New Spain!"[24]

At the time Calleja took office on March 4, 1813, Mexico City was divided into three factions — the *gachupines,* the insurgents, and the *callejistas.* Many Europeans regarded Calleja's wavering and uncertainty with suspicion, while the insurgents on the other hand viewed them only as evidence of his opportunism and concluded that his brutality would be no less severe than that of Venegas.[25] Calleja's conciliatory policy upon taking office was offered as proof of the arguments of *gachupines* and insurgents alike, for though the viceroy outlined an energetic program for crushing the rebellion and refused to restore freedom to the press, he nevertheless attempted to appease dissident groups by re-establishing the remaining portions of the suspended constitution and providing for the election of the *cabildo* of Mexico City.[26]

The election was held on April 4. Not a single European was chosen, although the Guadalupes reported that the viceroy and the archbishop exerted the greatest pressure to secure victories for their candidates.[27] Despite the defeat for the European party, Calleja announced that the elections for naming the individuals to compose the provincial deputation, together with those to represent Mexico in the Spanish Cortes would be held in July. "The election of the provincial deputation," wrote the Guadalupes, "is of the greatest importance, and we are working with every effort to insure that it will be composed of persons of our confidence."[28] Their labors were not in vain, for the outcome was another decisive victory for the Americans.

We took a great deal of interest in seeing that the election would bring victory to Americans of liberal ideas, sound qualities, and patriotic devotion [they reported to Morelos] and we have achieved that to our satisfaction in spite of our opponents, who made the greatest effort to influence the voting. Archbishop [Antonio] Bergosa [y Jordán] organized a large party, which worked with every means to influence the parish priests and ecclesiastics who served as electors for the provinces. Nevertheless, they conducted themselves with a heroism which we never expected. The viceroy worked no less energetically to achieve the success of his plans. . . .

On the next day, the election of the *vocales* to the provincial deputation was held. Mexico City was to elect two delegates and one *suplente* because Oaxaca is occupied by you. The most damaging blow was inflicted on our enemies, for [Miguel Gurudi y] Alcocer, ex-deputy to the Cortes, and José María Fagoaga, European by birth, but American by education and training, were elected. Chosen as the *suplente* was Licenciado Cristo [y Conde], who was born in Havana, and will perform his duties very well for us.[29]

The election of the deputies from Mexico to the Cortes held during that same month resulted in still another triumph for the insurgent party. Fourteen deputies and four *suplentes,* all of them American by birth, were chosen; but when Calleja declared that the government was unable to provide funds for their transportation to Spain, the representation from Mexico was reduced to two persons — José María Alcalá, canon of the metropolitan church, and Manuel Cortázar, a lawyer.[30]

Viceroy Calleja, in an *informe* to the Spanish government, made no attempt to minimize the importance of the victories of the revolutionary party during the first months of his administration.

At the present time [he began] two rebels who are acting in the capacity of deputies are en route to the Cortes; they are the *magistral* José de Alcalá and the lawyer Manuel Cortázar. Nowhere can there be such bitterness as my own in seeing two such pernicious subjects proceed to their destination without any obstacle so that they can dictate laws to the noble Spaniards and use the sovereignty of the metropolis to prepare and hasten the ruin of the Americas. . . . Since the rebels here are in continuous relation and agreement with their deputies in the peninsula, they understand what steps should be taken for America, and they demand compliance with their characteristic arrogance. . . .

The first popular election for the *cabildo* was the first triumph of the rebels . . .; the city was flooded with crowds of people, who carried torches all during the night; they shouted vivas to Morelos, to independence, and to the electors, all of whom were unreliable Americans, and most of them disloyal; they shouted death to the Europeans and to their government; they tried to break into the cathedral tower to ring the bells; and they had the audacity to appear before the palace and demand artillery. . . . Anyone can see the outlook with regard to the insurrection; but New Spain will not hang itself, nor refuse to obey its legitimate sovereign while I am alive and am responsible for its preservation, even though it should be necessary for the country to suffer blood and fire until the infamous are annihilated and the flag of the monarchy of Spain is planted everywhere. . . .[31]

One of the dominant themes in the correspondence of the Guadalupes with Morelos during 1813 was their insistence that the situation in Mexico City was ripe for his advance and that the strength of the revolutionary party within the capital was so great that only the news of the approach of the insurgent army was necessary to provoke a massive uprising which would overthrow Calleja's tyranny and deliver the capital to the invading revolutionary forces. One of their most interesting letters describes, and perhaps exaggerates, the status of revolutionary opinion and organization in the metropolis:

The party of true Americans inside Mexico City is very great, though its exact size cannot be estimated accurately. We cannot determine the allegiance of everyone in the capital, but we know that almost all the people aspiring to the aristocracy are so unprincipled by nature that there are only a few of them who could be called insurgents and who desire the liberty of their country. Most of them do not want to expose themselves to danger to contribute to the cause. . . . They often accept the tyranny which prevails, . . . and therefore this group cannot be of much use to us.

The common people automatically follow the first cry they hear. They do not look ahead; they never think of the future; they are content to live as dejected spirits as long as they are allowed to engage in vice. . . . Yet this class of people can be led easily, and some kind of party may be formed of them. The whole area of Mexico City is made up of this type, but their numbers lately have decreased greatly because of royalist recruiting parties, who want them for their regiments and because of the present epidemic which afflicts us.

The third class, or middle class, is not of the aristocracy nor of the common people. It is on the members of this class that we must depend largely for our support, for they are the ones who are most eager to sacrifice their lives for the cause. Their fear of the government's prisons and persecutions, and their dread of expressing their thoughts openly, have caused division among us, but that will not be the case when they hear you are approaching Mexico City, because all who have not declared themselves openly will join hands with our just cause.

We cannot say with certainty where the greatest number of true Americans are to be found within the city, but this will inform you that the whole area of the metropolis is filled with good Americans, and that your name is heard everywhere with the greatest rejoicing and enthusiasm. Only the center of the city is inhabited by *gachupines* and *chaqueta* creoles.[32]

But the plea of the Guadalupes, even if their information and judgment were reliable, went ignored and unheeded. Morelos was too busy during the first part of 1813 with the conquest of Acapulco, and too occupied the second half of the year with the organization of the revolutionary government to move as the Guadalupes desired. When he took the field again late in 1813 he suffered such disastrous reverses that the idea of attacking the capital ceased to be even a remote possibility.

REFERENCES

1. For details, see my article "Los Guadalupes: A Secret Society in the Mexican Revolution for Independence," *Hispanic American Historical Review*, XXX (November, 1950), 453-79.
2. "Informe del Exmo. Sr. Virrey D. Félix Calleja sobre el estado de la N.E., dirigido al Ministerio de Gracia y Justica en 18 de Agosto de 1814," Joaquín García Icazbalceta Collection, Latin American Collection, The University of Texas.
3. *Ibid.*
4. See Timmons, "Los Guadalupes," pp. 457-58, especially note 12.
5. Mora, *México y sus revoluciones,* IV, 194.
6. "Informe de Calleja sobre el estado de la N.E.," García Icazbalceta Collection, LAC UT.
7. Bancroft, *History of Mexico,* IV, 457-58.
8. Alamán, *Historia de México,* III, 280-82.
9. Genaro García (ed.), *Documentos históricos mexicanos,* III, introduction, pp. xvii-xx.
10. *Ibid.,* pp. xx-xxi.
11. *Ibid.,* IV, introduction, pp. xi-xii; J. M. Miguel y Vergés, *La independencia mexicana y la prensa insurgente,* pp. 171-76.
12. Alamán, *Historia de México,* III, 286-87.
13. Morelos to Rayón, Oaxaca, January 15, 1813, Hernández y Dávalos (ed.), *Colección,* IV, 818.
14. The Guadalupes to Morelos, Mexico City, December 7, 1812, Morelos Papers, LAC UT.
15. *Idem* to *idem, ibid.;* Nettie Lee Benson, "The Contested Mexican Election of 1812," *Hispanic American Historical Review,* XXVI (August, 1946), 336-39.
16. The Guadalupes to Morelos, Mexico City, January 20, 1813, Morelos Papers, LAC UT.
17. Proclamation to the inhabitants of Oaxaca, December 23, 1812, *Morelos documentos,* I, 150.
18. Part of the correspondence covering the negotiations was published in Castillo Negrete, *México en el siglo XIX,* V, 213-41. The rest is in manuscript form in the San Jacinto Museum of History, San Jacinto Monument, Texas,

under the title of "Papeles cogidos al rebelde Morelos sobre el estado de opinión y proyectos formados en esta capital en fines del año de 1812."

19. *Ibid.*

20. *Ibid.*

21. Morelos to Ignacio Ayala, Yanhuitlán, February 17, 1813, Hernández y Dávalos (ed.), *Colección*, IV, 859.

22. The Guadalupes to Morelos, Mexico City, January 20, 1813, Morelos Papers, LAC UT.

23. Bustamante, *Cuadro histórico*, II, 251.

24. Anastasio Zerecero, *Memorias para la historia de las revoluciones en México*, pp. 252-54.

25. The Guadalupes to Morelos, Mexico City, March 6, 1813, Morelos Papers, LAC UT.

26. Alamán, *Historia de México*, III, 409-410, 421.

27. The Guadalupes to Morelos, Mexico City, April 9, 1813, Morelos Papers, LAC UT.

28. *Idem* to *idem*, July 2, 1813, *ibid.*

29. *Idem* to *idem*, August 5, 1813, *ibid.*

30. Alamán, *Historia de México*, III, 422-23; Germán Latorre, "La separación del Virreinato de Nueva España de la metrópoli," *Revista de Archivos, Bibliotecas, y Museos*, XXXI (1914), 212.

31. "Informe de Calleja," LAC UT.

32. The Guadalupes to Morelos, Mexico City, August 5, 1813, Morelos Papers, LAC UT.

CHAPTER VIII

MORELOS' REFORM PROGRAM

IT will be remembered that Ignacio Rayón and the other members of the Supreme Junta, José Sixto Verduzco and José María Liceaga, had barely escaped to Sultepec after Calleja had defeated them at Zitácuaro in the early days of January, 1812. To regain lost prestige and, according to Alamán, "to consolidate and perpetuate the authority of the junta,"[1] Rayón drafted a constitution early in 1812, the first in the history of Mexico, inasmuch as the Spanish Constitution of 1812 did not go into effect until October of that year. Reflecting in some measure the ideas of Hidalgo, it declared that the Roman Catholic religion was to be the established faith of the state and that sovereignty, which emanated from the people, was to be vested in the person of Ferdinand VII but exercised by a supreme American national junta of five members elected by the provinces. A congress of representatives named for a three-year term by the property owners was to exercise the legislative power, but it was to be guided in its decisions by a council of state composed of all officers of the rank of brigadier and above. The constitution called for the establishment of four captains-general, including the three members of the junta, one of whom in time of war was to be chosen as temporary generalissimo with dictatorial powers. Moreover, the constitution contained numerous liberal features, such as freedom of the press, the right of habeas corpus, and the abolition of caste distinctions, slavery, and torture.[2]

On April 30, 1812, Rayón forwarded a copy of the constitution to Morelos for his comment and suggestions. Rayón received no reply, however, until early November. Although Morelos gave all sorts of excuses for his failure to answer, his delay was undoubtedly deliberate. By delaying he believed he could strengthen his own position: he was confident that his military fortunes would improve throughout the year, while those of the junta members would decline. That is precisely what happened. While Morelos was winning at Tehuacán and Orizaba, the operations of Rayón around Toluca and in the Tenango-Tenacingo area, and those of Liceaga in Guanajuato and Verduzco in Michoacán, resulted only in defeat and failure. By November, when Morelos finally framed his reply, he was in a far better position than any of the junta members to gain the post of generalissimo, should Rayón's document go into effect.

After indicating on November 2, 1812, that "the mask of independence must be removed inasmuch as the fate of our Ferdinand VII is now common knowledge,"[3] Morelos on November 7 forwarded a list of his objections to Rayón's constitution. First of all, the name of Ferdinand must be excluded, he said; any reference to his name was at that time "hypothetical." The council of state should be limited to a fixed number of officers because it would be very difficult to assemble all of those of the rank of brigadier and above should they be needed for consultation. Lastly, Morelos argued that the generalissimo should be elected for life and should hold office until incapacity, illness, or the age of sixty made further service impracticable.[4]

Whether Morelos' objections discouraged Rayón or whether he felt that the Spanish Constitution of 1812, which had been proclaimed in Mexico City in the meantime, eclipsed his own plan of government, is not clear, but his disgust with the whole project was fully apparent. He authorized Morelos to publish the constitution if he so desired, but concluded by saying that "we have done nothing except things to make us look ridiculous as if we were mere automatons."[5] Rayón's project never became law, though Morelos later made use of some of its provisions.

The great victory of Morelos at Oaxaca firmly established his reputation as foremost among the insurgent military commanders. As a result, though with some reluctance, Rayón's junta confirmed the appointment of Morelos as a fourth member of that body. The situation had changed since 1811, when he rejected the offer to serve on the junta and designated Verduzco to exercise the functions of membership for him. Now triumphant in 1812, Morelos decided that membership in Rayón's junta might be the most effective way to secure the adoption of his own political views and principles. As a matter of fact Morelos had already begun to press for the addition of a fifth member to the junta, even before his appointment as the fourth member had been confirmed.[6] It is interesting to note that Morelos' ideas respecting the method to be used in appointing the fifth member varied with circumstances — before the conquest of Oaxaca, Morelos was willing for the junta to make the choice, but after that victory he insisted that a citizen of the province of Oaxaca should be given the honor of membership and accordingly submitted a list of ecclesiastics with instructions for Rayón to choose one.[7] Quite naturally Rayón refused to bestow the office upon a person whom Morelos would completely dominate, and therefore countered by suggesting a candidate of his own. This move produced a stalemate between the two leaders, intensified their distrust of each other, and brought forth the charge from Verduzco and Liceaga that Morelos was a despot.[8] To make matters worse, Rayón's colleagues began to quarrel with one another, and the resulting charges and counter-charges produced what Castillo Negrete called "an unprecedented scandal" that did serious damage to the insurgent cause.[9] Each of the junta members appealed to Morelos for support, but received from him a reprimand instead. Maintaining a scrupulous neutrality, Morelos forwarded copies to Verduzco and Liceaga of the following note he addressed to Rayón:

Although you did not tell me in your last letter of the violent discord between you and the two other members, rumors about it have spread to the provinces, and it has been confirmed by the three couriers who arrived here today. Even though I read the letters of each one of you in the greatest secrecy, it has been impossible to conceal information concerning this catastrophe. I am thoroughly disgusted with everything. God grant that this cancer, which the enemy hopes for so much, shall not continue. Should all of us become involved in it, our perdition will be assured. I will sacrifice myself to obey the Supreme Junta, but I cannot give my support to any one individual for the purpose of destroying the others. . . . Furthermore, I will never accept a tyrannical government — that is, a monarchy, even though I should be elected sovereign. It is essential that we rule ourselves by a published constitution, so that the provinces will understand what a blunder all this dissension has been.[10]

On April 30, 1813, Morelos issued instructions for the formation of an elective assembly in Oaxaca to choose the fifth member of the junta, expressing at the same time the opinion that the total membership of the body should be increased to seven or nine.[11] Thus, the stronger Morelos' position became, the larger the number he recommended for junta membership. At length, an election held in Oaxaca in August named José María Murguía y Galardi as the fifth member, with Carlos María Bustamante receiving the second highest number of votes.[12] By now, however, Morelos had decided on an entirely new approach. So intense was his disgust with the junta, and so great was his desire for political stability, that he had already determined to convoke a national congress composed of representatives from the provinces for the purpose of completely reconstructing the insurgent government under his direction. Rayón might protest that such a body would be "lacking in authorization, prudence, and legality," and that Morelos' action was dictated by "vanity, adulation, and pride,"[13] but the complaints were meaningless, as Rayón himself knew, for his power was broken, and Morelos was master of the revolutionary movement.

In addition to his demand for the independence of Mexico, Morelos, while engaged in the conquest of the south, also proclaimed far-reaching social and economic reforms, which he hoped in time might be accepted as the program of the revolution and enacted into law by a stable insurgent government. Echoing some of the principles he had set forth earlier, Morelos demanded that the "very lovely conglomeration of social gradations" — Indian, mulatto, and mestizo — be abolished and all native-born persons be designated as "Americans." He insisted that sovereignty should reside in the people, but it should be exercised by a congress of Americans from which Europeans should be excluded. Since he believed that virtue was the only quality distinguishing men and their usefulness to state and church, Morelos called for the abolition of slavery, the tribute, and debts owed by Americans to Europeans. The lands should be owned by those who worked them, and the workers should receive the income from those lands.

All should work [he said] in that occupation which will render a person most useful to the nation. By the sweat of our brows we must work so that all of us will have bread to eat. The women should busy themselves in their own honest household labors; the priests must take care of souls; the laborers must be employed in agriculture, and the artisans in industry; the remaining men should devote themselves to the army or the government.[14]

The pro-Spanish historian Lucas Alamán, who rarely let an opportunity pass to discredit Morelos when he could, wrote in 1850: "The communists and socialists of our day, to whose systems Morelos leaned in a considerable degree, will recognize completely their principles in some of the points which he recommended to the Congress [of Chilpancingo]." "Since Morelos had come to regard the war as a struggle between proprietors and proletariat," continued Alamán, "there was attempted nothing less than the complete destruction of all property and the distribution of it among those who had nothing."[15]

The source for Alamán's charges is a celebrated document, which was undated and unsigned, though in all probability written by Morelos, entitled *Medidas políticas que deben tomar los jefes de los ejércitos Americanos para lograr sus fines por medios llanos y seguros, evitando la efusión de sangre de una y otra parte.* The subject of considerable controversy, it contains the following basic features:

1. All rich persons, nobles, and officials of the highest ranks, whether creoles or *gachupines,* will be considered enemies of the nation.

All their properties will be subject to confiscation, half going to the poor, and half to the army.

2. All properties will be taken as reimbursement.

3. The redistribution which will affect the people of the towns must be made with the greatest care, so that no one individual becomes enriched, and so that everyone in general is given assistance.

4. The same policy will apply to the properties of the churches, with the exception of parochial books.

5. Royalist buildings and archives will be burned.

6. Overseas products will be destroyed.

7. All haciendas greater than two leagues in size will be broken up into smaller plots.

8. Tobacco crops, mines, and sugar plantations will be destroyed.[16]

Much confusion has resulted because of the existence of two different texts of *Medidas políticas* — an abbreviated, incomplete copy drafted by a certain Juan Martiñena, and the complete text, copied by the royalist secretary Patricio Humana in October, 1814. Alamán admitted that he used only the Martiñena text with its numerous deletions and omissions; but an examination of the Humana text reveals without question that Morelos wrote the document when he was in the Tehuacán-Orizaba area in the fall of 1812, rather than in late 1813 in conjunction with the Congress of Chilpancingo, as Alamán states. Moreover, Morelos intended to set forth a military plan rather than a radical socio-economic program. The document was drafted at a time when Morelos was in desperate need of a military victory to strengthen his political position, and *Medidas políticas* should therefore be regarded as an aspect of his military preparations for the attack on Oaxaca. His immediate objective, he said, was "to destroy the tyrannical government and its satellites, check its greed with the destruction of the means by which it wages war, and strip the rich of the funds with which the government is supported."[17]

The points of *Medidas políticas* involving confiscation of properties, their redistribution, and the division of the large haciendas have caused many Mexican historians, especially in the present century, to hail Morelos as a pioneer agrarian reformer. To be sure, he did from time to time refer to the land problem, and on several occasions he recommended that those who worked the lands should be the owners and should receive the income from what they produced. He also suggested in the full Humana text that "there should be no one individual who should have a great expanse of unproductive land while thousands of people remain in a slave status. Instead, they should become free proprietors of a limited amount of land for the public welfare, as well as their own."[18] But these recommendations should be regarded as only means to an end rather than the end itself. His main purpose, from which he never deviated, was to annihilate the Spanish government and destroy its ability to make war. At no time did Morelos seriously consider a comprehensive agrarian program or submit one to the Congress of Chilpancingo.

The officials whom Morelos appointed to administer the finances of the insurgents were José María Murguía y Galardi, the intendant of the province of Oaxaca and subsequently the fifth member of Rayón's junta; Francisco de Pimentel, minister of the treasury; and José de Micheltorena, paymaster of the army. Morelos gave detailed instructions to these officials to be followed in their handling of insurgent funds. The instructions included the preparation of complete and accurate monthly reports of all receipts and expenditures.[19] Booty and the spoils of war provided much of the revenue. Oaxaca, for example, yielded three million pesos' worth of jewelry, cotton, and clothing, and proved to be Morelos' richest prize. Other revenues came from properties confiscated from Europeans. The insurgents swept aside the greater part of the taxes and duties of Spain's colonial administration, although they retained the *alcabala* (reduced from eight to four percent), the *diezmos*, and certain other parochial duties for the support of the clergy. Priests were to be exempt from payment of the tax on goods brought for their own personal use. The government monopolies on gunpowder and dyes were abolished, but all nitrates, sulphur, and gunpowder mined or manufactured had to be sold to the insurgent government.[20] Import duties constituted another source of revenue: Morelos declared that all goods entering ports under insurgent control were to be subject to a minimum ad valorem duty of twelve percent, which would never exceed one hundred percent. In administering finances Morelos was forced from time to time to resort to a *donativo*, or forced contribution on a product such as corn meal, to meet increasing governmental expenses, which in late 1812 were running to more than 1,500 pesos a day. When Morelos learned that certain merchants were fleecing insurgent officials and private citizens by charging exhorbitant prices for food and other necessities, he promptly issued a decree placing price ceilings on seven basic food commodities, as well as on soap, cigarettes, and candles.[21]

The financial difficulties of the insurgents were intensified by an annoying currency problem. Morelos had begun the issuance of a copper currency in 1811, and it was the only medium of exchange in use until after the capture of Oaxaca, when the coining of silver was begun. Although the insurgent mint at Oaxaca cast a large amount of silver, the supply of silver was far more limited than that of copper, with the result that there was considerable hoarding of silver coins by merchants, who refused to accept any other currency for their merchandise. Merchants carried off much silver currency to territories under royalist control. Counterfeiters made matters worse by adding spurious silver coins to the money supply.

There should be an increase in the coinage of silver and copper [suggested Francisco de Pimentel, the insurgent treasurer] and the hammer-struck coins should have a milled edge so that counterfeiting can be checked. . . . The silver supply which remains for coinage is very limited, and the hoarding of silver has forced people to pay a considerable price in copper to obtain it. Without silver one cannot find any grain or blankets to buy because the Indians refuse to carry the goods because of transportation difficulties and because they are not obligated to accept copper money. . . . The treasury should issue paper money in denominations of from five to a thousand pesos, leaving enough copper coins to facilitate small business transactions. Paper money would be easier to handle and more difficult to counterfeit. . . . We should also coin gold with the prescribed milled edges, because a considerable amount may be taken from the mines of Teoxomulco, Río de San Antonio, Texas, and Ixtepexi.[22]

No doubt Morelos made a strong effort to correct abuses and improve the financial situation of the insurgents, yet in the following statement to Carlos María Bustamante, he recognized that the problems were so great as to make a solution almost impossible.

At first I prohibited absolutely all trade [he declared] but later I issued an order that merchants from enemy territory could buy goods with silver only; then I ordered that conquered towns should pay for their wares with copper. Yet there are many transactions which are characterized by wickedness and the desire for personal gain.[23]

In the realm of ecclesiastical affairs Morelos found the Dean of the Oaxaca chapter, Antonio Ibáñez de Corvera, much more cooperative with the insurgent cause than Bishop Antonio Bergosa y Jordán had been. In the main, Ibáñez gave tacit consent at least to Morelos' use of the *vicario castrense*, or army chaplain, for the exercise of priestly functions and ecclesiastical duties for the insurgent army while it was on the march. In defining the ecclesiastical powers of the *vicario castrense*, Morelos and the insurgents made use of the privileges Clement X extended to chaplains in the bull of 1736, *Quoniam in Exercitibus*, which granted them the authority to assist in marriages, administer all the sacraments with the exception of confirmation and ordination, and to exercise all parochial functions.[24] The most active of the insurgent chaplains were José de San Martín, who had formerly served Bishop Bergosa, and José Manuel de Herrera, former *cura* of Huamuxtitlán, who joined Morelos at Chautla late in 1811.[25]

The personal correspondence between Morelos and Ibáñez de Corvera covered many topics both of an ecclesiastical and a political nature. There was much discussion of such religious matters as insurgent marriages, the nomination of ecclesiastics to parishes in need of spiritual guidance, the supplying of isolated parishes with sacramental necessities, burial rites and ceremonies for insurgents killed in battle, maintenance of discipline among the Oaxaca clergy, and the silencing of those European ecclesiastics who opposed the insurgent movement. Sometimes political and military affairs were discussed, such as the latest battlefield reports, insurgent military plans, the selection of the fifth member of Ignacio Rayón's junta, and the representatives of Oaxaca for Morelos' proposed insurgent congress.[26]

Like his predecessor Miguel Hidalgo, Morelos made extensive use of the name of the patron saint of the Indians, the Virgin of Guadalupe, to gain the support of the Indians for the revolution. Morelos, however, was far more aware than Hidalgo and others of the nationalistic influence which strong support of the Indian patron saint might lend to the revolution, and for that reason has been called the most outstanding of the insurgent leaders for his *guadalupanismo*.[27] There are a number of examples to support this conclusion. Early in 1811 after the occupation of the southern territory, Morelos established the province of Tecpán and named its capital Nuestra Señora de Guadalupe. On various occasions he preached sermons in honor of the Virgin. At Oaxaca, Morelos ordered a huge demonstration for the patron saint, and, according to an observer, as the church bells rang Morelos appeared in the window of the palace that overlooked the plaza, threw silver coins to the people, and ordered a procession of the groups from all the neighboring districts, each of which carried a standard bearing a most striking image of the Virgin of Guadalupe.[28] His decree of March 11, 1813, declared that

on the twelfth day of each month a special mass would be celebrated in all towns; on all balconies and in all doors there was to be placed an altar with an image of the Virgin, together with the necessary lights. All men ten years of age and over were to carry on their hats a badge with the national colors of white and blue, and a hat band on which they were to indicate their allegiance and devotion to the Virgin.[29]

The principal leaders of Mexican independence generally recognized the immense importance of the press as an instrument to disseminate information and propagandize the cause. Miguel Hidalgo established *El Despertador Americano* in Guadalajara; it published seven numbers during December, 1810, and January, 1811. José María Cos, an associate of Ignacio Rayón, founded *Ilustrador Nacional* in Sultepec in 1812, and made paper, ink, and all necessary equipment and tools with his own hands. After six issues had appeared, Cos suspended production, and started *Ilustrador Americano*, using a printer and a press that the Guadalupes of Mexico City had sent him. That same press also printed *Semanario Patriótico Americano*, edited by the distinguished Andrés Quintana Roo. Both papers were published in Sultepec until October, 1812, when they were moved to Tlalpujahua. Quintana Roo's paper lasted until January, 1813, while Cos' *Ilustrador Americano* appeared until April, 1813.[30]

Morelos may have started a press even before the conquest of Oaxaca and the subsequent founding of *Sud* and *Correo Americano del Sur* in that city early in 1813; the Guadalupe correspondence of October, 1812, refers to Morelos' "little press" and a printer they had hired for him.[31] But Morelos' printing operations did not begin on a large scale until after the conquest of Oaxaca, when he employed a printer named José María Idiáquez, and started work on a periodical called *Sud*. It is probable that only two issues of *Sud* had appeared, however, when Morelos began a far more ambitious project in founding *Correo Americano del Sur*, also printed by Idiáquez, who kept the paper going in spite of a "thousand obstacles."[32] The paper appeared throughout the greater part of 1813, first under the editorship of José Manuel de Herrera, and then, beginning in May, under Carlos María Bustamante.[33] Its stated objectives were to "counter-act the forces of deception," curtail "the prejudices of ignorance," cause the "light of wisdom" to shine, justify the cause, "glorify the noble partisans" of the revolution, confound the "haughty insolence" of the royalists, and "exalt the sentiments of patriotism to the utmost degree."[34] The *Correo* published news and information about the revolution, manifestoes and proclamations of the leaders, and detailed reports of insurgent victories.[35]

So far as is known, *Correo Americano del Sur* was the last insurgent periodical published in southern territory. In the fall of 1813 it was moved to Chilpancingo, where its press was used to publish the decrees and resolutions of the Congress. With the approach of royalist forces early in 1814, however, and after the attempt to move the press to Tlacotepec failed, it was captured by the army of José Gabriel de Armijo at Las Animas.[36] From that time on Morelos and the other insurgent leaders were pursued so fiercely by the royalists that little time remained for printing activities.

Whether Morelos' press-and-propaganda activities were as effective as he seemed to think is difficult to say; but perhaps he had reasons for believing that such efforts were a forceful weapon. "Circulate these numbers of *Correo Americano*," Morelos ordered Bustamante on one occasion, "and spread them throughout enemy territory so that the *chaquetas* may be swayed, and so that they may know the record of our achievements."[37]

Such, then, was the program of reform which Morelos developed and proclaimed in 1812. On completing the conquest of the south with the capture of Acapulco, Morelos was now ready to direct his attention and energies toward the establishment of a new insurgent government which would enact the program into law.

REFERENCES

1. Alamán, *Historia de México*, III, 546.
2. Rayón's constitution, in Hernández y Dávalos (ed.), *Colección*, VI, 200-202; see also Alamán, *Historia de México*, III, 546-49.
3. Morelos to Rayón, Tehuacán, November 2, 1812, Hernández y Dávalos (ed.), *Colección*, VI, 205.
4. *Idem to idem*, November 7, 1812, *ibid.*, IV, 662.
5. Rayón to Morelos, Puruarán, March 2, 1813, *ibid.*, VI, 206.
6. Morelos to Rayón, Oaxaca, December 31, 1812, *ibid.*, IV, 760.
7. *Idem to idem*, December 16, 1812, *ibid.*, p. 690; and *idem to idem*, December 31, 1812, *ibid.*, p. 761.
8. Morelos to Verduzco and Liceaga, El Veladero, March 28, 1813, Morelos Papers, LAC UT.
9. Castillo Negrete, *México en el siglo XIX*, V, 473.
10. Morelos to Rayón, El Veladero, March 29, 1813, Peñafiel, *Ciudades y capitales*, p. 117.
11. Morelos to Liceaga, El Veladero, March 29, 1813, Hernández y Dávalos (ed.), *Colección*, V, 5.
12. *Correo Americano del Sur*, No. 24 (August 5, 1813), in Genaro García (ed.), *Documentos históricos mexicanos*, IV, 185.
13. Diary of Ignacio Rayón, July 5, 1813, in *Apuntes para la biografía del Exmo. Sr. Lic. D. Ignacio López Rayón*, p. 35.
14. Decree of Morelos, Oaxaca, January 29, 1813, *Morelos documentos*, I, 156-57.
15. Alamán, *Historia de México*, III, 559, 575.
16. Alamán published the incomplete, abbreviated Martiñena text of the "Medidas políticas," which has stronger socio-economic overtones than does the complete Humana text, which sets forth a military plan. Although Hernández y Dávalos published both texts (the Martiñena copy carries Morelos' signature, while the other is unsigned), Mexican historians until recently have used the Martiñena copy almost exclusively, with the result that historians of the Díaz period condemn Morelos, while those of the Revolution praise him for his political and social radicalism. Still other Mexican historians, notably Ezequiel A. Chavez (*Morelos*, p. 206) have denied Morelos' authorship of the "Medidas políticas." Alfonso Teja Zabre has refuted this in his recent biography (*Vida de Morelos*, Chapter XX), and is probably closer to the truth than anyone else in his contention that the document was written by Morelos, and was intended to be a military plan of destruction and devastation. But the controversy over the document still rages.
17. "Medidas Políticas" (Humana text), Hernández y Dávalos (ed.), *Colección*, I, 220-21.
18. *Ibid.*
19. Decree of Morelos, San Pablo Huizo, February 10, 1813, *ibid.*, IV, 857-58.
20. Decree of Morelos, Oaxaca, January 29, 1813, *Morelos documentos*, I, 157.
21. Decree of Morelos, La Sabana, March 26, 1813, *ibid.*, pp. 158-59.
22. Report of Francisco de Pimentel, Oaxaca, July 8, 1813, Hernández y Dávalos (ed.), *Colección*, V, 79; see also Alberto Francisco Pradeau, *Numismatic History of Mexico*, pp. 100-117.
23. Morelos to Bustamante, Acapulco, August 23, 1813, Genaro García (ed.), *Documentos para la historia de México*, XII, 35.
24. *Semanario Patriótico Americano*, No. 22 (December 13, 1812), printed in facsimile in Genaro García (ed.), *Documentos históricos mexicanos*, III, 196; see also Cuevas, *Historia de la iglesia*, V, 88, note 17.
25. Alamán, *Historia de México*, II, 430; III, 327.

26. See, for example, Morelos to Ibáñez de Corvera, Oaxaca, January 18, 1813, Hernández y Dávalos (ed.), *Colección*, VI, 509.

27. Jesús García Gutiérrez, "El culto de la Virgen Santísima de Guadalupe durante la guerra de independencia," *Memorias de la Academia Mexicana de la Historia*, IV (January, 1945), 44.

28. Quoted in Cuevas, *Historia de la iglesia*, V, 83.

29. Decree of Morelos, Ometepec, March 11, 1813, *Morelos documentos*, I, 154-55.

30. Genaro García (ed.), *Documentos históricos mexicanos*, III, introduction, pp. xx-xxi.

31. The Guadalupes to Morelos, Mexico City, October 17, 1812, Morelos Papers, LAC UT.

32. Morelos to Bustamante, Chilpancingo, October 21, 1813, Genaro García (ed.), *Documentos para la historia de México*, XII, 49.

33. Genaro García (ed.), *Documentos históricos mexicanos*, IV, introduction, pp. x-xi.

34. *Ibid.*, pp. xi-xii.

35. See the analysis of the most significant numbers in J. M. Miguel y Vergés, *La independencia mexicana y la prensa insurgente*, pp. 171-76.

36. Joaquín Fernández de Córdoba, "Verdadero origen de la imprenta en Morelia," *Boletín de la Sociedad Mexicana de Geografía y Estadística*, LXII (July, 1946), 134-35; 185-87.

37. Morelos to Bustamante, Las Iguanas, May 8, 1813, Genaro García (ed.), *Documentos para la historia de México*, XII, 26.

CHAPTER IX

SERVANT OF THE NATION

JOSE MARIA MORELOS, priest, military commander, political and social reformer, principal leader of Mexican independence, and "Servant of the Nation," as he styled himself, was approaching his forty-eighth birthday as he completed the conquest of Acapulco and departed for Chilpancingo to organize the new national congress. There was little in his physical appearance to suggest greatness, for he was of small stature and stocky build; being only slightly more than five feet in height, and weighing perhaps 160 to 170 pounds, he was not particularly imposing in appearance. His facial features were rough and coarse, with warts and moles much in evidence, and there was a large scar scross his nose from a bad fall sustained in boyhood days. His coloring and complexion were dark; his skin and eyes were deep brown; and he had thick lips, and eyebrows which were heavy and joined. His body had been conditioned by a lifetime spent almost entirely in the field and outdoors, but he suffered greatly from malaria and migraine headaches. It has been suggested that the handkerchief he wore about his head, and with which he is almost always pictured, may have been worn to alleviate the pain from his headaches. But it may have been only to keep the hair out of his eyes or his brow free of perspiration. He suffered numerous injuries from accidents and falls: his correspondence from 1811 to 1813 makes frequent references to his maladies and general bad health.[1] He was constantly plagued with attempts on his life and threats to his person. He was twice warned that he was about to be poisoned,[2] and once Rayón wrote him that a man with a big belly was coming to seize him and turn him over to the viceroy. But this threat, like all the others, he received with his characteristic calm, and at the bottom of Rayón's note of warning, Morelos quipped: "There is no one here more big-bellied than I am, and my ailments are wearing me out."[3]

In a country which through its history has been plagued by ambitious men who have sought high positions solely for self-aggrandizement and personal glory and reward, Morelos was a conspicuous exception. It was characteristic of him, for example, to reject the title of Supreme Highness which the Congress of Chilpancingo sought to confer on him, in favor of the more modest one, Servant of the Nation. He was scrupulously honest, and though millions of pesos passed through his hands, he applied virtually all of the money to financing the revolution, keeping only small amounts to take care of his meager personal needs. A man of simple habits and tastes all his life, he loved hard work, expected it of his associates and subordinates, and scorned artificiality, sophistication, idleness, and vice. Aside from several indiscretions in his private life in violation of his priestly vows, his only indulgence was an occasional glass of *aguardiente* and a cigar.

I have tried to work with understanding [Morelos wrote to one of his officers] for the people have placed their fate in my hands. I cannot deceive them because a thousand hells would not be sufficient to punish me for my wickedness. It is not my wish to abandon them, nor to sacrifice them. I am a Christian, and I have a soul to save; therefore, I have sworn to sacrifice myself for my country and my religion before breaking my oath on a single point.[4]

The idea of calling a national congress of provincial representatives may have occurred to Morelos a month or so before he issued his decree of June 28, 1813, which set forth regulations for its formation. In April, it will be remembered, he had been willing for Rayón's junta to serve as a nucleus, with the total number increased to seven or nine, the additional members to be elected by the provinces.[5] But so great was his disgust with the continuous bickering and quarreling among Rayón and his associates that in May Morelos discarded his original plan in favor of a national congress of his own creation. He therefore suggested to Rayón that the five junta members should meet in Chilpancingo on September 8, 1813, and there its members "either were to be re-elected or removed," so that "individual differences could be eliminated."[6] Morelos was thus offering Rayón and his associates membership in the national congress, but only on condition that they would be willing to cooperate.

An insurgent congress was not a new idea in the era of Mexican independence, for Hidalgo had suggested one, as had Rayón in his constitution of 1812. But much of the credit for causing such a body to become reality belongs to Carlos María Bustamante, who convinced Morelos of the great need for it.

> Europe is aware of the justice of our revolution; [wrote Bustamante] the parliaments of London and the government of Washington eagerly desire to assist in a task where the oppression of humanity is involved, as well as to promote the trade and happiness of all states. They have not shown any generosity toward us, however, because an organization which should represent our will, and a means through which those powers could negotiate, is lacking. Favorable results have been obtained in Caracas and Buenos Aires because assemblies have been established there by reason of the desires of their political leaders, who have set an example for us in the organization of institutions which represent the sentiments of those peoples.
>
> America cannot be free as long as the provinces do not support this idea; foreign powers cannot recognize us as long as an august body where sovereignty may be deposited is missing. . . .
>
> The day of the bloody war — the war of the sword — has passed; we are about to enter into an era which will be characterized by cunning and diplomacy, and which will be extremely more dangerous than before. We should present, therefore to our oppressors a congress of learned men (Un Congreso de Sabios), so that we can win the respect of foreign powers and the confidence of the people of this continent.[7]

In a decree of June 28, 1813, addressed to the provinces, Morelos issued instructions for naming electors, who were to assemble in Chilpancingo on September 8, to select the members of the new congress. A subdelegate in each parish, it stated, should call together the *curas*, army officers, and principal citizens of each parish; and on a given day, they were to assemble in the provincial capital and select a representative by a plurality of votes.[8] Subsequently, Morelos declared that the executive power was to be exercised by a generalissimo, chosen from the four captains-general by insurgent officers of the rank of colonel and above, and approved by the congress.[9] This was the same arrangement Rayón had proposed in 1812, when no doubt he was thinking of holding the position himself, but now in 1813 the situation was vastly different from that of the previous year.

Morelos' measures were naturally opposed by Rayón as illegal and despotic, but his protests had little effect. Morelos countered that Rayón was only injuring the cause with his bickering, and proceeded to justify his own course in the following letter to his rival:

By your last two letters . . ., I can see that in your assumption of all of the powers under the pretext of saving the country, you desire only its death; you can see that it is in danger, but you try only to tie the hands of all its citizens, and to make it impossible for anyone to take the steps which are necessary. . . .

There arises the opinion, which you have formed unjustly, that the abrogation of your authority should be attributed to me, by virtue of the fact that I am favored with a preponderance of bayonets. . . .

The congress must be confirmed in Chilpancingo, God willing, in this coming month, and in any way possible, because I called it four months ago. By this act you will not be ignored; the country will not perish; neither will the said assembly lack legality, nor will it be ridiculed by our enemies, as you contend.

Let us not lose the means to free ourselves from our common mother, in order that your rights might be saved; the only other alternative is to declare the power which resides in your person illegitimate, because that which is reduced to personal ends cannot be legitimate; it only hinders the progress of the country in obtaining its independence.

I am opposed to pretentiousness; I will be content with any fate that will be useful to religion and in favor of my fellowman. I do not seek the presidency; my functions will cease when the congress is established; and I will restrict myself to the very honorable epithet of humble Servant of the Nation.[10]

The number of electors who had arrived in Chilpancingo by September 8, 1813, was disappointingly small. Since Morelos desired to proceed with the formation of the congress without further delay, he drew up on September 11 a *Reglamento*, or plan of government, composed of fifty-nine articles, which according to Bancroft, amounted practically to a constitution.[11]

Recognizing the principle of separation of powers, it declared that the executive authority should be exercised by a General-issimo, elected for life from the list of insurgent generals by a plurality of votes of the army officers holding the rank of colonel or above. The powers of the Generalissimo included the right to initiate legislation which he considered necessary to the public welfare. The legislative power was to be vested in a Congress, composed of *propietarios* chosen by the electors, and *suplentes* nominated by Morelos himself. Any *vocal*, or member of Congress, could propose projects for consideration, such proposals to become law with the approval of a majority of the members. Their terms were to be no longer than four years. Officials of the Congress included a president and vice-president, rotated among the *vocales* each four months, and two secretaries, to be appointed by Morelos for four-year terms. The judicial power was to remain vested for the time being in existing tribunals, but at some future date, there was to be a tribunal of five members for civil cases, and an ecclesiastical tribunal of from three to five to promote the welfare of the Church and decide cases involving the clergy.

The persons of the deputies were declared sacred and in-violable; deputies were not permitted to leave for military or other outside duties. Charges of disloyalty to country and religion on the part of any official were to be handled by a special junta of five persons elected by the five provinces nearest the seat of Congress. Finally, there was Article XVII — Morelos' recommendation for a declaration of independence from Spain without reference to any monarch.[12]

On September 13 at a meeting of the Tecpán electors held for the purpose of choosing their deputy to the Congress, Morelos' secretary, Juan Nepomuceno Rosains, read the *Reglamento;* and on the following day at a second meeting of the electors, together with certain officials and natives of Chilpancingo, Rosains read the celebrated document written by Morelos entitled "Sentiments of the Nation," which outlined his political and social program for the consideration of the Congress. Rosains also announced the names of those who were to compose that body. In the class of *propietarios* were the members of the old Supreme Junta — Ignacio Rayón for the province of Guadalajara, José Sixto Verduzco for Michoacán, and José María Liceaga for Guanajuato, as well as José Murguía y Galardi for Oaxaca (he had been chosen fifth member of Rayón's junta by an Oaxaca assembly), and José Manuel Herrera, who was chosen deputy for Tecpán by the electors of that province. Appointed as *suplentes* were Carlos María Bustamante for Mexico, José María Cos for Vera Cruz, and Andrés Quintana Roo for Puebla.[13] Since Morelos' Congress included those who had been members of the Supreme Junta, Rayón always considered it to be a mere extension of the earlier body. It will be noted also that Morelos named all of the deputies, with the exception of those from Oaxaca and Tecpán, and that there was hardly a chance in those two places for a candidate to be chosen who was not in sympathy with the Morelos program. In hand-picking his Congress, Morelos has been charged with failing to establish a democratic regime when he had every opportunity to do so. But this criticism is justified only so long as it can be assumed that Mexico was ready for democracy in 1813.[14]

The Congress was installed on September 14, and began its work with the consideration of Morelos' "Sentiments of the Nation." After declaring that "America is free and independent of Spain and any other nation, government, or monarchy," the "Sentiments" stated that "the Catholic religion shall be the only religion, without the toleration of any other," that its ministers should be supported by the *diezmos* and the first fruits, that the people should not be required to pay any obligations other than devotional contributions and gifts, and that the dogma should be sustained by the hierarchy of the Church, consisting of Pope, bishops, and *curas*, "because every plant which God did not plant should be pulled out."[15]

As to his political, social, and economic system, Morelos stated in the "Sentiments" that sovereignty emanated directly from the people but was deposited in their representatives, and that the powers of government should be divided into the legislative, executive, and judicial branches. Government offices should be held exclusively by Americans; no foreigners should be admitted other than artisans who were able to instruct in their professions.[16] Slavery was to be declared abolished, as well as all distinctions among classes. Laws should cover all except certain privileged bodies, because "the good law is superior to all men, and those laws which our Congress should enact should be such as to compel devotion and patriotism, regulate poverty and destitution, increase the wages of the poor, better his condition, and eliminate ignorance and violence." The ports of the nation should be open to friendly powers, but foreign merchants should not be allowed to go into the interior, nor should foreign soldiers be permitted on national soil. Property should be respected; torture should be abolished, as well as the *alcabala,* the monopolies, and the tribute. The war was to be financed with a duty of 10 per cent on imports, together with "another tax on foreign merchandise," a direct contribution of 5 per cent on rents, and careful administration of goods confiscated from the Europeans. Lastly, the day of December 12 should be celebrated in honor of the Virgin of Guadalupe, and September 16 should be solemnized as the anniversary of the beginning of the independence movement.[17]

After the installation of the members and the reading of the "Sentiments of the Nation," Morelos delivered an address entitled "Reasoning of General Morelos on the Opening of the Congress of Chilpancingo," which Carlos Bustamante had pre-

pared and sent to him from Oaxaca. Its most significant passages
are given here as follows:

Our enemies have been obliged to reveal to us certain important
truths; we were not ignorant of them, but the despotism of the government under whose yoke we have been oppressed attempted to
hide them from us. They are: that sovereignty resides essentially in
the people; that having been transmitted to monarchs, by their absence, death, or captivity, it falls back on the people; that they are
free to reorganize their political institutions in any way which is
agreeable to them; and that no people have the right to subjugate
another. . . .

These oppressed people, similar to the Israelites, who worked for
Pharaoh, are tired of suffering, and they lift their hands to the sky,
and make their clamoring heard before the throne of the Eternal.
Taking pity on their misfortunes, He opens His mouth and decrees
that Anahuac should be free. In the town of Dolores this voice was
heard, and it was like a thunderbolt. . . .

Spirits of Las Cruces, of Aculco, Guanajuato, Calderon, Zitácuaro,
and Cuautla! Spirits of Hidalgo and Allende should be witness to our
flood of tears! You, who govern this august assembly, accept the most
solemn pledge which we make to you today — that we shall die or
save the country. But we do not undertake or execute anything for
our own welfare if we do not decide beforehand to protect religion
and its institutions, to conserve properties, to respect the rights of
the people, to forget our mutual misunderstandings, and to work
incessantly for fulfilling these sacred objectives. . . . Spirits of Moctezuma, Cacamatzín, Cuauhtémoc, Xicotencatl, and Caltzontzín, take
pride in this august assembly, and celebrate this happy moment in
which your sons have congregated to avenge your insults. After
August 12, 1521, comes September 8, 1813. The first date tightened
the chains of our slavery in Mexico-Tenochtitlán; the second one
broke them forever in the town of Chilpancingo. . . . We are therefore going to restore the Mexican empire, and improve the government; we are going to be the spectacle of the cultured nations which
will observe us; finally, we are going to be free and independent.[18]

Meeting in the parish church on the next day, September 15,
the Congress designated José Sixto Verduzco as temporary
president, and considered the election of the Generalissimo,
who was to exercise the executive power. To the surprise of

no one, Morelos received the unanimous approval of the army officers of the rank of colonel and above and the subsequent approval of the Congress.[19] But when the position was formally offered to him, he refused to accept it, stating that he believed it to be superior to his capacity.[20] Some would argue that his rejection of the office was a feint on his part, caused by the fear that he would be accused of being power thirsty; but it is more likely that he was motivated by genuine abnegation and a sincere desire to indicate that he had not created an executive position in the expectancy that he was to fill it. Moreover, he may have been uncertain of his support, and therefore may have delayed to ascertain how much of a following he had before he accepted. President Verduzco and the army officers declared that Morelos should be forced to accept to satisfy the unanimous desire of the people, while Quintana Roo insisted that Congress should avoid hasty action and take more time for deliberation. The dispute was settled only when it was suggested that the Congress should adjourn for two hours and then announce its verdict. On the passage of the motion, Morelos retired to the sacristy of the church and smoked a cigar while he waited.[21]

At the expiration of one hour the members entered the sacristy and presented Morelos with a document which stated that they had conducted deliberations with the people of the town, to whose acclamations they had acceded in declaring that Morelos' renunciation was inadmissible. The Supreme Congress, it continued, in the exercise of its sovereign powers, would compel his immediate acceptance of the position, recognize him as the first military chief, and reserve the right to dictate the title which it chose to give him.[22] "Thus," wrote Lucas Alamán, "was the legislative power subdued before military force. Sad presage of fate which awaited future congresses!"[23]

Morelos replied that in view of the public demonstrations and his respect for the authority of the Congress, he would accept, with four conditions: first, that should the troops of a

THE STATESMAN

foreign power invade the country, they should not be allowed to approach the seat of the Congress;[24] second, that on his death, command should devolve temporarily on the military chief next highest in rank until an election should decide the permanent successor; third, that the Congress must not deny him assistance in money and men which he might need, nor exempt any privileged classes from service; and fourth, that in the event of the death of the Generalissimo, the unity of the army and the people should be maintained, and established authorities recognized.[25]

After the Congress had accepted these conditions, Morelos assumed command, taking an oath "to defend at the cost of his life the Catholic religion, the purity of the Most Holy Mary, the rights of the American nation, and to discharge to the best of his ability the office which the nation had conferred on him." Rosains then took the oath as secretary to the executive power, and the session of September 15 closed by rendering thanks to the Supreme Being with a solemn Te Deum.[26] The Guadalupes of Mexico City sent congratulations, adding that a number of delegates who had been elected to the Cortes of Spain had voiced a preference for serving in the Congress rather than in the illegitimate assembly at Cádiz.[27]

It was more than a month, however, before the Congress could open for regular business, since Rayón, Bustamante, Liceaga, and Cos were still absent. Morelos continued to inform them of developments and urge their presence in Chilpancingo, but it was late October before all had arrived. Meanwhile, Morelos in his capacity as Generalissimo retired the three members of the Supreme Junta from command with the rank and honors of captains-general without salary;[28] he then appointed Mariano Matamoros as commander-in-chief for the provinces of Tecpán, Oaxaca, Mexico, Puebla, and Vera Cruz; and Manuel Muñiz as commander-in-chief for Michoacán, Guanajuato, Guadalajara, Zacatecas, and San Luis Potosí.[29]

The Congress, having been assured by October 25 that all members would likely arrive, made preparations to hold regular sessions, fixed the hours for meeting, and declared that any individual had the right to submit any plan or project for congressional consideration, and that he might attend the sessions if he desired.[30] By the end of the month all members had taken their seats, except Rayón, who on the last day of the month appeared at the nearby hacienda of Chichihualco. He was received by a body of officials sent by the Congress under Antonio de Sesma, and was escorted to Chilpancingo in great pomp and ceremony on November 2. Quintana Roo and others were on hand to welcome him to Chilpancingo, and on November 4, after he had been administered the oath of office, Rayón took his seat in Congress.[31]

The Congress took up for discussion Morelos' "Sentiments of the Nation" and decided that the first order of business should be a declaration of independence from Spain. Morelos addressed the body and read a proclamation he had written entitled "A Short Plea which the Servant of the Nation makes to his Fellow-Citizens."

We are free by the grace of God [it began] and we are independent of the arrogance and tyranny of Spain, with her extraordinary Cortes, which is so lacking in reason. . . . Europeans, do not burden yourselves any longer creating petty governments. America is free, even though we do not seem to be. . . . I have spoken to you in simple and intelligible words; heed this advice and understand once and for all that although he who speaks to you may die, the nation will not change her system for many centuries.[32]

On November 6 the Congress approved Carlos María Bustamante's draft of a declaration of independence in spite of the protests of Rayón, who insisted that Hidalgo's fall was caused largely by desertions which came as the result of too much talk about independence. Rayón declared that there was still considerable respect for Ferdinand VII, particularly among the Indians, who had been accustomed for so long to venerate monarchy.[33] Nevertheless, the Congress ordered that Bustamante's document be published without further delay; it then drafted a manifesto to enlist the support of the Mexican people for independence and the revolutionary effort. Significant portions of Bustamante's Declaration of Independence are as follows:

The Congress of Anáhuac, legally installed in the city of Chilpancingo, of America Septentrional by its provinces, solemnly declares in the presence of God, judge and moderator of dominions, and author of society, who creates those dominions and removes them according to the unalterable designs of His disposition, that under the present circumstances in Europe, it has recovered the exercise of its usurped sovereignty; that in view of this, Spain remains defeated forever, and therefore the dependence on the Spanish throne should be dissolved; that it is the judge of the establishment of laws which are necessary for better government and domestic happiness, for making war and peace, for establishing alliances with monarchies and republics of the old continent, as well as for celebrating concordats with the Highest Roman Pontificate for the rule of the Apostolic Roman Catholic church, and for sending ambassadors and consuls; that it does not profess nor recognize any religion other than the Catholic, nor will it tolerate or permit the use of any other in public or in secret; that it will protect with all its powers the purity of the faith and its dogmas, and the preservation of the regular orders. . . .

There followed a statement that the Congress would consider anyone guilty of high treason who should oppose directly or indirectly the independence of Mexico which had thus been declared.[34]

If Morelos expected the Congress to proceed with the confirmation of his social and economic program at Chilpancingo, he was to be disappointed. Other than adopting a decree abolishing slavery and one restoring the Society of Jesus for educating youth in Christian doctrine and propagating the faith in the frontier regions, little was done.[35] But the cornerstone of a Mexican nation had been laid at Chilpancingo; and perhaps in time the Congress would incorporate the Morelos program in a written constitution for an independent Mexico. The completion of the structure, however, required that the insurgents gain additional victories on the battlefield. Thus the year 1814 promised to be a critical one for the Mexican revolution now being waged for the declared purpose of independence.

On November 7, 1813, the day after Mexican independence was proclaimed, Morelos and his army set out for Valladolid, the place of his birth, and the cradle of the revolution.

REFERENCES

1. See, for example, Morelos to the Junta of Zitácuaro, Acahuizotla, September 27, 1811, in Alamán, *Historia de México*, II, 424.
2. The Guadalupes to Morelos, Mexico City, October 24, 1812, Morelos Papers, LAC UT.
3. Quoted in Alamán, *Historia de México*, II, 425-26.
4. Morelos to Ignacio Ayala, Yanhuitlán, February 17, 1813, Hernández y Dávalos (ed.), *Colección*, IV, 860.
5. Morelos to Liceaga, El Veladero, March 29, *ibid.*, V, 5; decree of Morelos, Acapulco, April 30, 1813, *ibid.*, p. 42.
6. Morelos to Rayón, Acapulco, May 18, 1813, *ibid.*, IV, 925.
7. Bustamante to Morelos, Oaxaca, May 26, 1813, *ibid.*, V, 50-51.
8. Decree of Morelos, Acapulco, June 28, 1813, *ibid.*, p. 133.
9. Decree of Morelos, August 8, 1813, *Morelos documentos*, II, 164.
10. Morelos to Rayón, Acapulco, August 5, 1813, Hernández y Dávalos (ed.), *Colección*, V, 99-100.
11. Bancroft, *History of Mexico*, IV, 564-65.
12. *Reglamento* of Morelos, Chilpancingo, September 11, 1813, *Morelos documentos*, II, 165-72, *passim*.
13. Sentiments of the Nation, Chilpancingo, September 14, 1813, *ibid.*, pp. 174-75.
14. Alberto María Carreño, "Los primeros pasos hacia la democracía y la independencia mexicanas (1810-1813)," *Memorias de la Academia Mexicana de la Historia*, III, (1944), 67.
15. Sentiments of the Nation, Arts. 1-4, *Morelos documentos*, II, 175.
16. Arts. 5-10, *ibid.*, p. 176.
17. Arts. 11-23, *ibid.*, pp. 176-77.
18. Discourse of Morelos, Chilpancingo, September 14, 1813, *ibid.*, pp. 177-81.
19. See list of army officers who voted for Morelos, *ibid.*, pp. 185-87.
20. Session of September 15, 1813, *ibid.*, p. 182.
21. Bustamante, *Cuadro histórico*, II, 385.
22. Session of September 15, 1813, *Morelos documentos*, II, 183.
23. Alamán, *Historia de México*, III, 563.
24. Alamán thinks that this probably was because of insurgent fear of a repetition of what had taken place in Texas when Gutiérrez de Lara was deprived of his command by Alvarez de Toledo, assisted by adventurers from the United States. See *ibid.*
25. Session of September 15, 1813, *Morelos documentos*, II, 184.
26. *Ibid.*
27. The Guadalupes to Morelos, Mexico City, November 3, 1813, Morelos Papers, LAC UT.

28. Morelos to Rayón, Chilpancingo, September 18, 1813, Hernández y Dávalos (ed.), *Colección*, V, 166.

29. Decree of Morelos, Chilpancingo, September 18, 1813, *Morelos documentos*, II, 188.

30. Decree of the Congress, Chilpancingo, October 25, 1813, *ibid.*, p. 193.

31. Diary of Rayón, *Apuntes para la biografía de Rayón*, pp. 40-41.

32. Proclamation of Morelos, Tlacosautitlán, November 2, 1813, *Morelos documentos*, II, 191.

33. Germán Latorre, "La separación del virreinato de Nueva España de la metrópoli," *Revista de Archivos, Bibliotecas, y Museos*, XXXI (Sept.-Dec., 1914), 222.

34. Declaration of Independence, Chilpancingo, November 6, 1813, Hernández y Dávalos (ed.), *Colección*, V, 214.

35. See the facsimile of the edict abolishing slavery in Julio Zárate, *La guerra de independencia*, p. 408; Bustamante, *Cuadro histórico*, II, 407.

CHAPTER X

MORELOS IN DECLINE

MORELOS' great desire to conquer Valladolid was based in part on sentiment, as well as on practical military considerations. Since the city was the place of his birth and the cradle of the revolution, it seemed fitting that the new insurgent government should be established there; moreover, his military information had convinced him that the city was inadequately defended and could be taken readily without great losses.[1] Without revealing his plans, Morelos, in the capacity of Generalissimo, summoned Nicolás Bravo, Hermenegildo Galeana, and Mariano Matamoros to hasten to Chilpancingo with their forces, and ordered various other commanders to protect the Congress and to maintain insurgent control around Oaxaca and Acapulco.

On November 7, the day following the promulgation of the Declaration of Independence, Morelos left Chilpancingo, proceeded in the direction of Tlalchapa, Cutzamala, and Huetamo, through that part of the *tierra caliente* he had known so well in former days as a priest, and arrived at his parish of Carácuaro in the first week of December.[2] It was his first visit in more than three years, and his heart was moved, writes Bustamante characteristically, when his eyes fell upon his old parishioners, the parish house where he had lived, and the church which he had built with his own hands. Here he remained for several days, occasionally stopping before an image of the Lady of Guadalupe to pray for victory on the forthcoming venture.[3]

From Carácuaro the insurgents passed to Chupio and Tacámbaro, arriving on the outskirts of Valladolid on December 22. By that time Morelos had assembled the largest army he commanded during his entire career, well equipped with provisions and thirty cannon, and numbering more than six thousand men.[4]

On the other hand, the Valladolid garrison, commanded by Domingo Landazuri, numbered only about eight hundred men, and Morelos lost no time in warning the royalists that he would transform the city into a "theater of horror," and its plazas and streets into "rubbish piles," if the place were not surrendered within three hours.[5] He also sent a letter to Abad y Queipo, Bishop-elect of Michoacán, denouncing him as an "agent of tyranny," censuring him for fulminating excommunications against the insurgents, and holding him responsible for the evil which would fall on Valladolid should he refuse to deliver the city.[6] The defenders of the city, however, ignored all demands. As a result, Morelos gave the order to attack, directing the brunt of the insurgent fire against the Zapote gate.

But Morelos had not reckoned with Calleja's ability and energy employed during 1813 to revitalize the royalist effort. While the insurgents were bogged down in the long, drawn-out siege of Acapulco, and while their leaders indulged in petty quarreling as they attempted to form an insurgent government at Chilpancingo, Calleja effectively reorganized the royalist forces, aided by troops recently released from duty in Spain. Having been informed by November 24 of Morelos' movements toward Valladolid, Calleja ordered Ciriaco Llano and Agustín de Iturbide to move by forced marches in defense of the capital of Michoacán. As a result, reinforcements numbering more than three thousand men arrived in time to check the insurgent assault on the Zapote gate, throw back the troops of Bravo and Galeana in disorder and with great losses, and then enter the city in triumph.[7] This was a terrifying shock to the insurgent leadership, which was unaccustomed to such reverses; Morelos was stunned, and Nicolás Bravo cried like a baby.[8]

At length, Morelos placed Mariano Matamoros in command of insurgent forces, and plans were made for another attack on the city. But before the insurgents could advance, Iturbide attacked. Bustamante writes that the royalists had intercepted an order from Morelos instructing all men below the rank of captain to paint their faces black so they would not be mistaken for the enemy; whereupon the defenders blackened the faces of several hundred of their forces and marched out of the city as night was coming on, Iturbide leading the vanguard.[9] Royalist charges threw the insurgents into such confusion that the latter began killing one another, since they were unable to distinguish friend from foe. Panic spread through their ranks, and they fled in all directions. The aspirations of the insurgents and the prestige of Morelos had received a damaging blow.

After the disaster at Valladolid, Morelos retired to Chupio, collected some of his scattered units and marched toward the hacienda of Puruarán, twenty-two leagues southwest of Valladolid, with the forces of Iturbide and Llano in hot pursuit. Perhaps Morelos was too eager for a chance to avenge the catastrophe at Valladolid, for in spite of the warnings of his officers, who urged him to continue the retreat, he decided to make a stand. By the morning of January 5, 1814, the forces of Llano had overtaken the insurgents, and although their resistance was valiant, the royalist artillery scored with telling effect. The battle was over in half an hour. The insurgents were put to flight and driven into a river, where they were cut down by the hundreds. Although the material losses suffered by the insurgents were overwhelming, they were nothing compared with the capture of Mariano Matamoros, whom Bustamante called Morelos' left arm, Galeana being the right.[10] The prisoner was led to Pátzcuaro, placed on exhibition in the plaza, and made to suffer countless indignities as he was brought to Valladolid. There he was tried, degraded, and sentenced to be shot. Although Morelos made a desperate effort to obtain Matamoros' release by offering Calleja two hundred Spaniards in exchange, the sentence was carried out as scheduled two days before Morelos' proposal reached the capital. It probably would have been rejected anyway. Today, a plaque which hangs on the veranda of the Hotel Antonio de Mendoza in Morelia marks the place of execution.[11]

From Coyuca, Morelos continued his retreat to Ajuchitlán, on the right bank of the Mescala. There he was able to collect approximately a thousand men who had fled after the disasters at Valladolid and Puruarán. He named as his second-in-command the ambitious Juan Nepomuceno Rosains, much to the disgust not only of Galeana, who was by far the ablest of Morelos' officers, but also of the Congress, which objected to the appointment to high military command of a man almost completely lacking in training and experience. Morelos moved on to Tlacotepec and joined the Congress early in February.[12]

Meanwhile, no sooner had Morelos left for Valladolid in November, 1813, than the contentious spirit among the members of the Congress broke out again. Under the leadership of Ignacio Rayón, who had consistently held that this body was only an extension of the Supreme Junta, the members assumed the executive power and attempted to take over the direction of insurgent governmental affairs.

After Morelos had been defeated in Valladolid [wrote Rosains in his *Relación*] all strength disappeared; all feeling was lost; the opinions of Congress were divided; and the legislative and executive powers fought one another. Men were entrusted with military command who had no experience in exercising it, and a force strong enough to keep them in check was lacking. Each one set aside a territory, made himself master of it, fixed taxes, filled offices, usurped property rights, and took lives. Passions were unleashed; liberty was confused with license and libertinage; and insurgent territory became a chaos of horror and confusion.[13]

As the advancing royalist army of José Gabriel de Armijo approached Chilpancingo, the Congress was forced to flee, and from that time on, it was an itinerant body, pursued relentlessly from place to place by the viceroy's armies. After Rayón, Bustamante, and Crespo retired to Oaxaca, the remaining five — Verduzco, Cos, Herrera, Quintana Roo, and Liceaga — fled to Tlacotepec on January 22, 1814. There Morelos, in disgrace and humiliation, readily surrendered the executive power, and though he retained his title of Generalissimo, he was prohibited from exercising military command over any forces other than his personal escort, which numbered about one hundred fifty men.[14] The Congress placed military authority in the hands of three commanding generals — Rayón, Cos, and Rosains — who were assigned to the provinces of Tecpán and Oaxaca, Michoacán and Guanajuato, and Puebla and Vera Cruz, respectively. The Congress also assumed political authority and promptly voted to increase its membership to sixteen.[15] Thus, in February, 1814, Morelos held only an empty military title and a seat in the Congress as deputy for Nuevo León; whereas four months before, in September, 1813, his political and military supremacy was unchallenged.

The advancing Armijo could not be stopped. So narrow was the escape of the Congress from Tlacotepec on February 24, that the royalists captured the archives of the Congress, its seal, the correspondence of the Guadalupes, the famous Oaxaca oil painting of Morelos, numerous other personal items (such as his uniforms, sword, and baton), and a number of things which had belonged to Matamoros.[16] After ordering Morelos to the Acapulco area to dismantle the port before it fell into royalist hands, the five remaining members of the Congress fled to the northwest, where they remained in Uruapan for about three months. Perhaps the real reason for sending Morelos to the south coast was to get him out of the way for a while.

At a meeting of Morelos and Galeana at Tecpán, there was so much emotion that Bustamante writes he could not hold back the tears when he heard the details. The two leaders discussed the recent disasters, and Galeana declared that he had become so discouraged that he had decided to abandon the cause and spend the rest of his days in hiding. "All has been lost," he confided to Morelos, "because you have entrusted men to the command of arms who are not deserving of it. I do not know how to write, it is true, but I can attack a camp as well as anyone." Then Morelos tried to console him; he reassured him of his sincere friendship, and urged him to continue fighting for the cause.[17] Galeana agreed that he would, and the two parted company. Morelos left for Acapulco, while Galeana remained in the area of Tecpán to attack small parties of royalist troops and destroy their supplies. But in a clash near Coyuca, on June 27, Galeana's forces were routed; and in the confusion which followed, Galeana's spirited horse ran under a tree and struck his rider's head against a low branch with such force that the impact threw him unconscious from his saddle to the ground. A royalist soldier then came up to administer a final blow, decapitating the fallen hero. When Morelos received the news, he was horrified: "Both of my arms are gone," he said; "now I am nothing."[18]

The port of Acapulco had suffered considerably from inefficient administration and mismanagement from the time it passed under insurgent control in August, 1813. It was reported in January, 1814, that the food problem was so critical, the armament so inadequate, and disease so rampant, that the defense of the fortress was almost impossible.[19] Therefore, when Morelos heard that Armijo was approaching, he retired to Pie de la Cuesta nearby, and gave orders to Isidoro Montes de Oca, on April 9, to reduce the port to ashes.[20] Four days later Armijo arrived to find that the place was in ruins, and that Morelos had fled to Tecpán. With Armijo in pursuit, Morelos retired to the northwest, moving along the coast through Petatlán and Zacatula, and leaving a trail of bloody reprisals in his wake as his answer to the execution of Matamoros.[21] This route was the same he had taken three and a half years before in October and November, 1810, just after he had joined Hidalgo, except that now the direction was reversed. And, it may be added, so also were the circumstances.

In the comparative seclusion of the ranch of Atijo, which had been a part of Morelos' ecclesiastical jurisdiction when he was *cura* of Carácuaro, he remained with his escort until the summer. In subterranean passages under a hill, so it was reported in 1815 by José María Morales, chaplain of the Congress, Morelos imprisoned those ecclesiastics who had incurred his wrath, the most important being Pedro Ramírez, an Augustinian, who had been chaplain of Acapulco. Ramírez had agreed to cooperate in espionage activities for the insurgents, but the Guadalupes of Mexico City revealed that after his arrival there, he had become a spy for Viceroy Calleja. Ordered by the viceroy to conduct espionage activities among the insurgents, he was promptly seized and imprisoned by Morelos.[22]

Meanwhile, the insurgent movement had suffered severe reverses in other sectors of Mexico. It will be recalled that when the Congress stripped Morelos of his military power, it entrusted Ignacio Rayón with the defense of Tecpán and Oaxaca, Juan N. Rosains with Puebla and Vera Cruz, and José María Cos with Michoacán and Guanajuato. Rayón set out for Oaxaca, stopped at Huajuapán, and dispatched José de San Martín to supervise the city's administration and organize the defenses. Insurgent rule had become so inefficient and unpopular, however, that when a royalist force under Melchor Alvarez descended upon Oaxaca, the city fell without a shot being fired in its defense. Subsequently, royalist control was restored throughout the entire province.[23]

Developments among the insurgents in Puebla and Vera Cruz were marked primarily by a shameful quarrel between Rayón and Rosains. When the insurgent Congress at length determined to put an end to their scandalous conduct by entrusting Francisco Arroyave with provisional command over the territory in dispute, Rosains had him apprehended and shot. As a result, most of those like Guadalupe Victoria who had served Rosains loyally, deserted him in disgust. A similar conflict developed in Michoacán and Guanajuato between Manuel Muñiz, appointed by Morelos in September, 1813, and José María Cos, named by the insurgent Congress. The struggle, however, never reached the proportions it did elsewhere and it largely died out in the summer of 1814 when Cos surrendered his military authority to devote his entire time to legislative matters.[24]

Significant developments had been taking place in Spain in the meantime. The defeat in 1813 of the French forces at Victoria and Salamanca by the combined Anglo-Spanish armies under the Duke of Wellington marked the beginning of the end of French rule in Spain. The liberated Ferdinand VII, in March, 1814, crossed the Pyrenees and, encouraged by the recent Bourbon restoration in France, the imposing strength of the party of reaction in Spain, and his warm reception as he made his way back to the capital, proceeded to "turn back the clock" to the absolutism of former days. The Cortes was dissolved, and the institutions of the old regime were re-established, including the Inquisition. A decree of May 4, 1814, restored political affairs to their pre-1808 status and declared all intermediate legislation null and void, including, of course, the Constitution of 1812.[25]

Ferdinand's restoration and the return of absolutism were received with solemn and imposing celebrations in New Spain, but genuine enthusiasm was lacking. For the moment the restoration tended to consolidate the insurgent effort and divide the royalists. While a conservative faction welcomed the return to reaction, a liberal faction, on the other hand, distressed over the repudiation of constitutional rights, began to look in the direction of the insurgents. Cos and Rayón, in particular, addressed appeals to the liberal party,[26] and Morelos urged everyone to repudiate Ferdinand, who, he insisted, was still being dominated by Napoleon, whom Morelos despised.[27] But the military fortunes of the insurgents had deteriorated to such a degree that Viceroy Calleja was able to act with determination and decision in preventing the breach within royalist ranks from becoming serious. He threatened the wavering with decrees to shoot all who should take up arms against the government, and offered pardons and generous terms to those who would lay down their arms, including Morelos and the other leaders, on condition that they would leave the country. But Morelos regarded the offer as only a trick, and wrote Nicolás Bravo instructing him to tell the people to reject it as a false and deceitful measure.[28] Nevertheless, Calleja's efforts were in general successful, and the insurgents, as Bancroft points out, "saw with apprehension one group of adherents after another dropping off, with a corresponding decline in their resources."[29] As a result, the idea of a written constitution as an expedient to combat the viceroy's efforts and to revitalize a dying cause became apparent to the insurgent leadership, which began to concentrate its efforts in that direction in the summer of 1814.

During May and June, 1814, the Congress continued to flit from place to place, not only to escape the viceroy's forces but, it would seem, to avoid Morelos as well. From Tiripitío, on June 15, the Congress issued a manifesto announcing its determination to continue the struggle, ridiculing the viceroy's charge of discord within insurgent ranks, and stating that work had begun on "a sacred letter of liberty," which would serve as a "lasting monument to convince the world of the dignity of the object to which our steps are directed."[30] Morelos, some distance away at Agua Dulce, replied to the Congress in his characteristic manner:

I should say to this body that there is nothing which I am forced to add to the manifesto. . . : first, because it has said everything; and second, because when the master speaks, the servant should keep quiet. This is what my parents and teachers taught me. You should be satisfied with my good behavior, especially with respect to my service to the country. It is well known that after I left the coast, I changed my march three times in search of the Congress to discuss the salvation of the nation in complete accord, and that I suspended my march because of illness contracted in the service of my country; and thus I was deprived of seeing you. Let them say how much wickedness they desire; let them resort to every perversity; I will never change from the system to which I have sworn; neither will I become involved in a discord, which I have tried to avoid so many times. My labors will support these truths, and I will not delay in exposing the impostors, because there is nothing hidden which is not found, nor secret which is not known.[31]

At length the Congress retired to the relative safety and seclusion of Apatzingán, where, after about four months' labor, the Constitution of 1814 was completed and proclaimed on October 22, 1814. It declared that its "sublime object was to free the nation from foreign domination, and to substitute for the Spanish monarchy a system of administration whereby the nation might enjoy its august and imprescriptible rights." In the greatest of solemnity, members of the Congress took an oath to the new instrument of government, celebrated a mass of thanksgiving, and sang a Te Deum. Festivities in a lighter vein followed, and all the members embraced each other and danced with joy, as did Morelos, who forgot his usual reserve for the moment.[32]

The Constitution of Apatzingán, which provided for a republican form of government in 242 articles, was signed by the following eleven members of the Congress: José María Liceaga for Guanajuato, José Sixto Verduzco for Michoacán, José María Morelos for Nuevo León, José Manuel Herrera for Tecpán, José María Cos for Zacatecas, José Sotero de Castañeda for Durango, Cornelio Ortiz de Zárate for Tlaxcala, Manuel de Alderete y Soria for Querétaro, Antonio José Moctezuma for Coahuila, José María Ponce de León for Sonora, and Francisco Argandar for San Luis Potosí. Although Carlos María Bustamante, Ignacio Rayón, and Andrés Quintana Roo did not attend the session, they forwarded their suggestions and ideas, and perhaps had a greater influence on the final document than any of those at Apatzingán. Contrary to the general impression, the influence of Morelos was negligible. Judging from a statement which he made during his trial to the effect that he read the document hurriedly and signed only because he believed it to be the best that could be drafted under the circumstances, he may not even have arrived in Apatzingán until the Constitution was nearing completion.[33]

It is apparent that the framers of the Constitution were inspired by a vast and varied number of sources, including Spanish colonial law, the French constitutions of 1791 and 1795, the Spanish Constitution of 1812, and Rayón's plan of government of 1812. Some provisions, according to Morelos, were borrowed from the Constitution of the United States, although the influence of that document seems slight.[34] The most significant features of the Constitution of 1814 include: popular sovereignty, separation of powers, the Catholic religion as a state faith, a weak plural executive, a powerful national legislature, and an indirect system of elections. In providing for the cumbersome executive of three persons, who were chosen by the legislature, and the prohibition against any governmental official exercising military command, the document reveals an intense fear of one-man rule. Since Morelos had consistently favored a strong executive and a dependent legislature, he termed the Constitution of 1814 "impracticable," and said in 1815 that experience indicated that it contained many errors.[35] Yet it should be pointed out that the Constitution of 1814 was intended to be provisional only, and was not without merit in many respects. It lifted insurgent morale; it gave legality and dignity to the insurgent regime, particularly in the eyes of foreign powers; and it demonstrated the faith of the insurgent leaders in the ultimate triumph of their cause.[36] It alarmed Viceroy Calleja to the degree that to counteract its influence he issued the most drastic measures in retaliation. In that policy, moreover, he was supported by the Inquisition, which charged that the Constitution of 1814 was heretical, and which made liable to the penalty of excommunication anyone who should have it in his possession.[37]

A significant beginning was made in the matter of establishing the new constitutional government with the election of the plural executive in the persons of Morelos, Cos, and Liceaga. The last named was to serve as the first President for a term of four months. Members of the supreme tribunal were also appointed; but in accordance with a constitutional provision,

the existing Congress was to continue to function as the legislative power so long as the provinces of Mexico remained under
royalist control. As it had done before, the Congress assumed
its customary role as a mobile body, fleeing from place to place
during 1815, barely managing to stay one step ahead of the
pursuing royalist forces, and finally coming to rest at Uruapan.
There, in the latter part of the summer, the three branches of
the government, with the exception of Cos, who was absent
from the executive power, were re-united.[38]

On August 30, Cos, who rather consistently entertained lofty
notions of exercising military command, issued a proclamation
condemning the Congress as an illegitimate body, and raised
the standard of revolt in an effort to overthrow it. The Congress
promptly dispatched Morelos to seize the upstart, and to shoot
him if he resisted. No sooner had Morelos appeared on the scene
than Cos' followers deserted him, and he was "apprehended
without the loss of a drop of blood."[39] Brought back to Uruapan,
he was tried and sentenced to be shot, though the Congress
declared the sentence would be mitigated if he showed some
evidence of remorse. But Cos remained adamant, even when
his casket was brought into the room for him to see. Just then,
the clergy of Uruapan and a group of people burst into the
room, fell on their knees, and begged that Cos be spared. Among
the group was Nicolás Santiago Herrera, *cura* of Uruapan, "the
venerable Herrera," as he was called. He had held his post
for twenty years or more and was the same ecclesiastic whom
Morelos had served as a teacher of grammar and rhetoric in
1797. Cos' sentence was commuted to life imprisonment in the
subterranean passages of Atijo, where he remained until liberated by a counter-revolutionary movement two years later.[40]

Because of the ever-increasing royalist pressure, the security
of the Congress became more uncertain. Therefore, in the
interest of greater safety, and for the purpose of placing the
government closer to the eastern ports of Mexico where assistance expected from the United States could be received, the

Congress voted to move eastward to Tehuacán. The execution
of this daring project, which involved escorting the Congress
to its new home, was entrusted to Morelos. Before the story
of that adventure may be told, however, it is necessary to
summarize the heroic but futile efforts of the insurgents to
obtain help from the outside.

REFERENCES

1. Testimony of Morelos, *Morelos documentos*, II, 352.
2. Bustamante, *Cuadro histórico*, II, 409-410.
3. Bustamante, *Elogío histórico del General Don José María Morelos*, p. 20.
4. *Ibid.*, pp. 20-21; Testimony of Morelos, *Morelos documentos*, II, 352.
5. Morelos to the commander of the Valladolid garrison, December 23, 1813, Hernández y Dávalos (ed.), *Colección*, V, 249.
6. Morelos to Manuel Abad y Queipo, December 23, 1813, Castillo Negrete, *México en el siglo XIX*, VI, 104-105. The original of this letter is in the San Jacinto Museum of History.
7. See correspondence of royalist commanders in *Morelos documentos*, I, 69-83.
8. Bustamante, *Cuadro histórico*, II, 416-17.
9. *Ibid.*
10. *Ibid.*, p. 423.
11. Morelos to Viceroy Calleja, Coyuca, January 24, 1814, *Morelos documentos*, II, 279-280. Alamán's charge that Matamoros made a formal retraction before his death is challenged by José de la Fuente, who presents convincing evidence that the retraction was written by Abad y Queipo. See his "Matamoros," *Anales del Museo Nacional*, IV, 348-49.
12. Testimony of Morelos, *Morelos documentos*, II, 353-54.
13. *Relación histórica de lo acontecido al Lic. D. Juan Nepomuceno Rosains como insurgente*, introduction, Juan E. Hernández y Dávalos Collection, Expediente 16-7, No. 3664.733, Latin American Collection, University of Texas.
14. Testimony of Morelos, *Morelos documentos*, II, 354.
15. Manifesto of José María Cos, Cienaga, March 1, 1814, Hernández y Dávalos (ed.), *Colección*, V, 296-97; Alamán, *Historia de México*, IV, 33-34.
16. See documents in *Morelos documentos*, II, 211-14; 227-29.
17. Bustamante, *Cuadro histórico*, III, 13.
18. *Ibid.*, pp. 80-83.
19. Patricio Fernández Giráldez to Morelos, Acapulco, January 30, 1814, *Morelos documentos*, II, 201-203.
20. Manifesto of Morelos, Acapulco, March 26, 1814, Morelos Papers, LAC UT; Morelos to Montes de Oca, Pie de la Cuesta, April 9, 1814, Alamán, *Historia de México*, IV, 65, note 45. The original of this letter is in the San Jacinto Museum of History.
21. Testimony of Morelos, *Morelos documentos*, II, 353.
22. Testimony of José María Morales, *ibid.*, p. 378.
23. Morelos to Nicolás Bravo, Agua Dulce, August 26, 1814, José L. Cossío (ed.), "Una carta inédita del Cura Morelos," *Boletín de la Sociedad Mexicana de Geografía y Estadística*, LXII (September-October, 1946), 330.
24. Alamán, *Historia de México*, IV, 114, 119.

25. Bancroft, *History of Mexico*, IV, 595-97.

26. Proclamation of Cos, Taretán, July 19, 1814, Hernández y Dávalos (ed.), *Colección*, VI, 227-28; Proclamation of Rayón, Zacatlán, August 19, 1814, *ibid.*, V, 610-13.

27. Testimony of Morelos, *Morelos documentos*, II, 360.

28. Morelos to Nicolás Bravo, Agua Dulce, July 23, 1814, *ibid.*, p. 264. The date is incorrectly published as 1811.

29. Bancroft, *History of Mexico*, IV, 600.

30. Manifesto of the Congress, Tiripitío, June 15, 1814, Hernández y Dávalos (ed.), *Colección*, V, 543-44.

31. Morelos to the Congress, Agua Dulce, June (?) 15, 1814, *ibid.*, p. 544.

32. Preamble to the Constitutional Decree for the Liberty of Mexican America, Apatzingán, October 22, 1814, *ibid.*, p. 703. Alba and Rangel (eds.), *Primer centenario de la Constitución de 1824*, has the Constitution of 1814 and an excellent analysis of it by Julio Zárate. See also Bustamante, *Cuadro histórico*, III, 204-205.

33. Testimony of Morelos, *Morelos documentos*, III, 30.

34. Manifesto of the Congress, Apatzingán, October 23, 1814, Hernández y Dávalos (ed.), *Colección*, V, 721-22; Testimony of Morelos, *Morelos documentos*, III, 29-30.

35. *Ibid.*, p. 30.

36. Herbert I. Priestley, *The Mexican Nation*, p. 326.

37. Alamán, *Historia de México*, IV, 176-78.

38. *Ibid.*, pp. 276-83, *passim*.

39. Proclamation of Morelos, Zacapo, September 7, 1815, Morelos Papers, LAC UT.

40. Luís Páez Brotchie (ed.), "Documentos relativos al insurgente Dr. José María Cos," *Memorias de la Academia Mexicana de la Historia*, I (1942), 265-82.

CHAPTER XI

THE QUEST FOR FOREIGN AID

FROM the earliest days of the Mexican struggle for independence, the leaders of the insurgents adopted, as had the Patriots in the American Revolution, the realistic view that the final victory could not be won without substantial assistance from one or more foreign powers. Although the Mexican insurgents carried on some negotiations with Great Britain, their greatest effort was directed toward the United States, which was involved in the War of 1812 with Great Britain from June, 1812, to December, 1814. As one might imagine, the period of the most intensive diplomatic activity of the insurgents in their search for aid came at the time the Morelos movement was declining most rapidly.

Hidalgo made two attempts to secure help from the United States, both of which failed. Pascasio Letona, it will be remembered, was commissioned to negotiate a treaty of alliance and commerce with the United States but was apprehended before he left Mexico. In 1811 Ignacio Aldama was ordered to Texas to get help, but he arrived at San Antonio de Bejar just as a counter-revolutionary movement was in progress, and was promptly seized, tried, and shot.[1]

Morelos' first attempt to obtain aid came soon after he learned of the capture of Miguel Hidalgo. In the early part of the summer of 1811 Morelos ordered David Faro, a survivor of the Philip Nolan expedition who had distinguished himself in the fighting around Acapulco, and Mariano Tabares, a native of that port, to journey northward for the purpose of negotiating "an alliance with the United States."[2] In a letter written on February 17, 1813, Morelos revealed to one of his officials that he had considered the situation so serious in 1811 that he was prepared "to cede the province of Texas" to the United States in return for assistance.[3] The two men started out, it will be remembered, but were stopped by Ignacio Rayón, who had just assumed the leadership of the Hidalgo movement. Instead of allowing the two men to proceed, Rayón gave them military commissions and ordered them to return to the south. When Morelos refused to recognize their commissions, they attempted unsuccessfully to sabotage the revolution. It is interesting to speculate on the probable outcome of the negotiations, had they been conducted; for after the purchase of Louisiana, a lively interest, both official and unofficial, had developed in the United States concerning the Spanish territories which lay on both sides of Louisiana — West Florida on the one hand, and East Texas on the other.

On August 27, 1812, Morelos addressed a letter to Holmes Coffin, captain of the British frigate *Aretusa*, which was anchored at Antón Lizardo near the island of Sacrificios, explaining that an insurgent captain named Agustín Niño had told him that the British commander was interested in negotiating a commercial treaty. An enclosure addressed to "The Admiralty, or to the Ministers of Great Britain" stated that the insurgents would pay cash for guns, pistols, and saber blades.[4] After considerable delay the British commander finally replied, on December 13, that the information Morelos had received was false, and that he, the British official, had no authorization from his government to negotiate a commercial treaty. But he stated that he would be glad to offer his services in bringing about a reconciliation between insurgent and royalist forces fighting in New Spain.[5] Morelos did not even bother to answer. He may have suspected that the commander was working for the Spaniards, and that any reconciliation would be prejudicial to the insurgent cause. At any rate, one week after the British commander replied to Morelos, he turned over to the Spanish governor of Vera Cruz all his correspondence with the insurgents.[6]

Morelos in 1815 suggested to another British naval commander the possibility of negotiations, but quite understandably this move came to nothing. The naval officer promised that he would try to induce his government to furnish troops and arms if Morelos would pay the millions of pesos which the merchants of Cádiz, Vera Cruz, and Mexico City owed the British![7] Since there was little chance that Morelos would assume responsibility for the debts of any Spaniard, it is not surprising that he announced, early in 1813, that he was directing his efforts toward the United States, and that he was seeking a commercial arrangement whereby grain and other products of Mexico could be exchanged for guns from the northern country.[8]

Morelos' conviction that help could be obtained from the United States was in all probability based on information he had received from a young revolutionary in New Orleans named Simón Tadeo Ortiz de Ayala. According to his own story Tadeo Ortiz was a creole of Guadalajara, who had left Mexico in 1810 to continue his education in Europe. After the Napoleonic wars interrupted his plans and the French prevented him from returning to his native land, Tadeo Ortiz escaped to the United States with the intention of entering Mexico through Texas. In Philadelphia in 1811 he met José Alvarez de Toledo, a former deputy from Santo Domingo in the Spanish Cortes, who had championed the American cause with such enthusiasm that he was forced to flee from Cádiz. Alvarez de Toledo arrived in Philadelphia in September, 1811, determined to foment a revolutionary movement in the provinces of northern Mexico.[9] It was not long before the activities of the two men had aroused the suspicions of the Spanish ambassador to the United States, Luis de Onís, who wrote the commander at Nacogdoches on December 21, 1811, as follows:

There has arrived in this city [of Philadelphia], coming from Cádiz, a youth named Don Tadeo Ortiz, native of Guadalajara of this kingdom. His conduct here has been very suspicious, for he has joined with the fugitive ex-deputy of the Cortes, Don José Alvarez de Toledo, who has published a burning and libelous denunciation designed to discredit the legitimate government and to promote insurrection in Spain's dominions in America. Tadeo Ortiz is going to New Orleans, and I am assured that he carries papers written by insurgents in Spain for *Cura* Hidalgo and the other revolutionary leaders there. I have advised the Spainsh consul in New Orleans to watch his behavior and to keep you advised. . . . I will give him a passport, but instead of having the customary signature, it will have a mark under the word "gratis," so that you may identify this suspicious individual. Don Tadeo Ortiz is twenty-two years of age, of slender build, medium stature, dark complexion, with black hair and eyes. Do not be surprised if some papers of Toledo are found among those carried by Ortiz. . . .[10]

Tadeo Ortiz arrived in New Orleans early in 1812, remained in that area for more than a year, and lost no time in establishing contacts with the Mexican insurgents — Morelos, Rayón, and the Guadalupes of Mexico City. A copy of the manifesto of Alvarez de Toledo which Luis de Onís had mentioned was forwarded by Tadeo Ortiz to the Guadalupes, who sent it to Morelos. Although the following letter from Tadeo Ortiz to Morelos was intercepted, it is typical of several which undoubtedly reached insurgent hands. This one, dated New Orleans, June 18, 1812, is as follows:

The American nation is powerful and respected. It will be able to give all the necessary aid at the moment that a deputy with the proper credentials presents himself, and whenever a point by land or sea is secured for the establishment of communications. It appears that this nation will declare war against Britain. This will be very important for us and our cause, for this nation will give not only arms, but even troops if necessary, as well as vessels for our ports and coasts. The political aims of this government with respect to the Spanish American nations include alliances with them as soon as they become independent, for in this manner, they will gain greater respect from Europe. I am informed that this government is disposed to give help in the form of a promise, if it cannot be it in any other way, providing that there is a government, even a temporary one, with which it can deal. It states that while one is not established there is not much hope for the successful results which it desires. . . .

Everyone desires a point by sea or by land so that they can communicate with Mexico. You should devote most of your attention to this matter. If that point is obtained, it will decide the issue of independence, for in that way we can introduce arms and everything else which is necessary, all of which this country has in great abundance. Moreover, a deputy should be sent to start negotiations. He not only should be wise, prudent, judicious, but affable, courteous, and well-educated. He should have full powers to deal with the agents of foreign governments which desire our friendship. I consider myself unworthy of such a post, but I have friends who are experienced in matters of diplomacy who hold me in esteem. If the matter of sending a deputy is approved, I would be deeply grateful if you did not forget me for one of the inferior commissions. I am not desirous of power; I wish to serve my country.[11]

Morelos delayed his reply for more than a year, probably because he was awaiting the outcome of developments in Texas, where royalist forces had crushed two attempts to overthrow viceregal authority in the period from 1810 to 1813.[12] Therefore, when Morelos received news of a third overwhelming insurgent failure in Texas, this time sustained by Tadeo Ortiz' friend, José Alvarez de Toledo, he decided to send Tadeo elsewhere to secure help for the Mexican revolution. According to the account of this youthful revolutionary idealist, he was commissioned by Morelos late in 1813 as diplomatic agent to New Granada to obtain weapons, boats, financial assistance, and a treaty of alliance. Tadeo Ortiz embarked at New Orleans, and before he arrived at Cartagena a year later, he had encountered and survived one harrowing experience after another, vividly described in his "Relación general de mi viaje."[13] He was almost always without money; frequently he was without food; he was sick much of the time and almost died once; he was in prison for a period of time; and his adventures involved him in a countless number of scrapes in Cuba, Santo Domingo, Haiti, and Jamaica. In Port au Prince he decided to burn his personal papers, including his diplomatic credentials and orders, to prevent them from falling into enemy hands. By preserving fragments of the documents to aid his memory, he planned at some later date to draft facsimiles of the originals. One of the documents which he reconstructed in that way was his commission to New Granada, dated "Guaxaca," November 29, 1813, and signed by "Manuel Morelos, General in Chief of Mexico." It is given here as follows:

I have received two letters from you dated New Orleans whose contents give me much joy, not only because of the news you sent, but also because of the information that there are patriots in the United States of such great merit, and that they may be as useful as our needs demand. Your observations gave me much joy, as did the commission which you requested. Considering the good which will come to Mexico, and the great service which you can make for our country, I did not hesitate a moment to commission you Agent of Foreign Affairs and Provisional Deputy relating to the Independent Governments of Meridional America, especially when I heard such good reports about you and your family.

The many affairs and difficulties, however, did not provide me a secure means of sending you your commission, nor the funds with which to carry it out. At that time I was waiting for results from the province of Texas, for I had utilized the means of communicating with that province so that I could send associates to you with sufficient powers and money to fulfill their commissions with ability and honor. The misfortune in the above-mentioned province, however, caused me to change my plans, and because I took the port of Acapulco a short time later, I decided to try to communicate with Panama and the provinces of Popayán and Quito in the belief that they had been taken over by the new kingdom of Granada. The lack of ships did not permit me to obtain any information on that matter, and since I lacked news from those parts, I lost hope of carrying out my project for a direct and safe means of communication so that I could send you funds.

Adjusting myself to the critical circumstances, however, I have decided to grant you provisional powers, and to name you Agent of Foreign Affairs and Provisional Deputy to the Independent Governments of Caracas and the new kingdom of Granada. I am sending you a letter for the leaders of those republics, together with powers, credentials and instructions which you will observe in every treaty and agreement made with those governments, or with any other friends of our independence.

The principal aim of your commission is to solicit the friendship of those countries, to establish communication, to inform them of the state of our revolution, and to obtain their resources for the formation of an expedition of their privateers so that we can receive their help and establish commercial relations with them. . . . We hope that they will give us a loan to the credit of the Mexican government, and that they will send us 15,000 guns, if it is possible, by way of the South Sea, or by the North Sea to the port nearest our provinces of Tabasco or Yucatán; but if the said governments do not furnish the said loan, or cannot use the ports of the South Sea, we hope that they will give you enough for a trip to North America or to the European colonies in America. Please report to me with regard to your acceptance of these powers, your time of departure, and anything in general regarding your affairs which can be communicated to me.[14]

Tadeo Ortiz at length, in late 1814, arrived in Cartagena, as the revolution in New Granada was at ebb tide. He made his way to Tunja and Santa Fé de Bogotá, and addressed a large volume of correspondence to Simón Bolívar, pleading for an audience and a chance to present his case. But the revolutionaries of New Granada viewed his credentials with suspicion and concluded that he was a spy. Bolívar could have done little for his Mexican revolutionary brothers anyway, for he was being pursued relentlessly by the forces of General Pablo Morillo. At length, Tadeo Ortiz was captured, and until he returned to his native land in 1822, he remained outside the main stream of events in Mexico.[15]

Although the Guadalupes continued to insist during the latter part of 1813 that assistance was imminent,[16] Morelos was not so optimistic. In those dark days of 1814 he called on his Anglo-American compatriot and expert on gunpowder, Peter E. Bean, and ordered him to the United States "to bring on a campaign against the province of Texas, and . . . to make some provision for a supply of arms."[17] Bean relates how he left Oaxaca with two thousand pesos and journeyed to Tehuacán, where the people there raised ten thousand more for him. He proceeded to Puente del Rey, remained one night in the camp of Guadalupe

Victoria, and continued on to Nautla, a little town on the coast north of Vera Cruz. There he found an abandoned schooner, which he attempted to make seaworthy enough for a trip to New Orleans. He watched a fight a short distance offshore between a British brig and the *Tigre,* a privateer which had as one of its passengers Joseph Amable Humbert, a veteran of the Napoleonic wars and an ambitious pirate. The *Tigre* vanquished its foe, but the crew got so drunk in celebrating the victory that the craft was beached about six miles north of Nautla. Bean hastened to the scene, found some of his friends on board, learned that the Spaniards at Vera Cruz had promised the British captain two thousand pesos to capture the schooner, and discovered for the first time that the United States and Great Britain were at war. Bean sent for his schooner and transported everyone, including Humbert, to Nautla.[18]

When Humbert arrived in Nautla, the insurgent commanders hailed him with great delight. They apparently thought he could help them and little suspected that he was only a pirate.[19] He came at the time when the quarrel between Rayón and Rosains over the military jurisdiction of Vera Cruz was at its height; so when Bean set sail for New Orleans on his schooner, Father José Antonio Pedroza who supported Rayón, and Juan Pablo Anaya who supported Rosains, prepared to leave for New Orleans with Humbert on the *Tigre.*[20]

New Orleans, which had been under the American flag for a little more than a decade, was still a frontier outpost beyond the furtherest reaches of law and order, and the ordinary processes of civilization; therefore it was still a favorite hangout for the restless, the adventurous, the scheming, the intriguing, and the rebellious. Moreover, in the months after Bean and the others arrived in New Orleans in September, 1814, there was even more restlessness and excitement in the air than usual because of the preparations for defense that General Andrew Jackson was making against the anticipated British invasion.[21]

Factors of self-interest and personal rivalries nullified much of the effort to get help for the Mexican revolution. Humbert had never been anything other than a pirate who was seeking opportunities to advance himself. Father Pedroza disagreed with and opposed Anaya. Moreover, in November, another person injected himself into the picture — one who was well known to New Orleans and the Louisiana frontier, José Alvarez de Toledo.

The activities of the Mexican insurgents in New Orleans were suspended with the landing of British forces, but they were promptly resumed after the American victory on January 8, 1815. Bean, Anaya, and Toledo began to cooperate to some extent in formulating plans which would help the Mexican revolution. In February, 1815, Toledo established contact with the Mexican Congress and revealed his plans. He had several hundred men under arms in preparation for an attack on the northern frontier of Mexico, and he had enlisted the services of an excellent sea captain, Julius Caesar Amigoni, who agreed to maintain communications between New Orleans and Mexico. The insurgent Congress, on the other hand, was expected to furnish funds, letters of marque, officers, and above all, an experienced diplomat with powers to conclude a treaty with the United States and to deal with foreign nations. Copies of Toledo's plan were addressed to the Mexican Congress, to Morelos, Rayón, and Cos. Bean was ordered to carry the letters to Mexico aboard Amigoni's schooner, the *Aguila*, to proceed to Nautla, establish contact with the Congress, and return as soon as possible with the funds and the diplomatic agent.[22]

Bean set sail from New Orleans late in February, arrived safely in Nautla, and set out with six companions on a journey of six hundred miles through enemy territory to meet with the insurgent Congress. Bean found Morelos at the hacienda of Puruarán, and recorded the interview in his Memoir as follows:

Morelos asked me what good news I brought from the United States. I related to him how I got there, and what I had done. I told him the United States was our friend and well-wisher; but since it was at war with Great Britain at the time, it might not be able to do much for us. It was then agreed to send an ambassador to the United States, and that I should return with him. 25,000 pesos was all the money that could be raised for the purpose.[23]

In the meantime, Anaya had fallen into Toledo's disfavor and had left for Mexico late in March, accompanied by John Hamilton Robinson, a St. Louis physician, who had been active in the Southwest since his days with Zebulon Pike. Although José María Morales, the chaplain of the insurgent Congress who was later captured and tried with Morelos, declared that Anaya had brought three hundred muskets to Mexico,[24] Morelos denied the story, and said that Anaya had never been able to accomplish anything. Morelos also declared that he considered Robinson either as an oddity or a spy, inasmuch as he had a passport but no credentials. He added, however, that he had issued Robinson a commission to take Pensacola in the name of the revolution, and had given him a thousand pesos for expenses, but that the results of the expedition were still unknown to him, since Robinson had not left Huetamo until the middle of October, 1815. Morelos concluded his declaration by affirming that during the whole course of the revolution no arms or munitions had been received from the outside. Questioned a second time with particular reference to the weapons brought by Anaya, Morelos answered with a flat denial.[25] Unfortunately for the insurgents, since they did not receive the military supplies, Morelos did not have to hide the truth.

In compliance with Toledo's request, as conveyed by Bean, for the insurgent government to appoint an emissary to the United States, the Congress, on July 14, 1815, commissioned José Manuel Herrera as minister plenipotentiary, and granted him ample powers and instructions to negotiate with the United States.[26] He set out from the hacienda of Puruarán for the Vera Cruz area on July 16, accompanied by Bean, Francisco Antonio Peredo, Cornelio Ortiz de Zárate, and Juan Almonte, Morelos' thirteen-year-old son, who was being sent to the United States for his education.[27] Herrera encountered so many difficulties on his trip to the coast that he was at the point of giving up the undertaking when there arrived at the port of Boquilla de Piedras the *Petit Milan* (*Aguila*), carrying Alvarez de Toledo, some Americans, and a cargo of military supplies. Toledo's purpose in coming to Mexico, according to the letters which he wrote on July 24 to Bean, Rosains, and Guadalupe Victoria among others, was to avoid any further delay in getting the Mexican diplomat and funds to New Orleans. Herrera agreed that if the cargo was unloaded at Boquilla de Piedras, he would pay for it on his arrival in New Orleans. Although Herrera did not suspect as yet that he was going to be trapped, he began to get very uneasy about the 29,000 pesos the Congress had given him and his companions to finance Toledo's expedition.

The voyage to New Orleans was long and rough, and Herrera was considerably relieved when he arrived safely on November 1 after a stormy month at sea. As soon as he landed, he had to surrender 23,000 pesos in payment for the cargo; and for future shipments of munitions and supplies, for which the Americans charged outrageous prices, Herrera spent the rest of his money. He then had to write the Congress for an additional 100,000 pesos to finance Toledo.[28]

Soon after his arrival in New Orleans, Herrera was inducted into the filibustering clan and informed of projects of conquest beyond the Sabine. Those plans usually included the capture of a Mexican port to facilitate communications with New Orleans and to serve as a base for pirateering operations, which were to be coordinated with expeditions by land and supplemented with reinforcements brought by ship to Matagorda or La Bahía. One such expedition did arrive at Galveston; but when a second expedition was wrecked in attempting to land, and when additional reinforcements failed to appear, the enterprise collapsed.[29]

Judging from Herrera's correspondence, he planned from the time he first arrived in New Orleans to undertake a trip to Washington to present his credentials and inquire about the possibility of obtaining aid, but he was constantly frustrated in his efforts by various filibustering projects. Probably because he received news late in December of the capture of Morelos, he decided to abandon the idea altogether and return to Mexico. He therefore addressed the following note to James Madison, President of the United States:

On the first of November last, I reached this city with the intent of remaining here only the time absolutely necessary to make preparations for continuing my trip to Washington, and placing my credentials in the hands of Your Excellency; but I was frustrated in my intentions and hampered in my movements. I have spent four months in New Orleans, and the obstacles which delayed my departure have grown more and more numerous. This unpleasant situation has induced me to return to Mexico.[30]

Herrera, however, remained in New Orleans a while longer, and made a pretense of keeping open the port of Galveston to assist a Mexican republic which had become almost non-existent. Within a short time José Alvarez de Toledo, who for many years was the recognized leader of the filibustering fraternity of the Louisiana frontier, announced his determination to seek the pardon "of his beloved monarch, Ferdinand VII,"[31] and thus betrayed the insurgent cause as he had betrayed his king five years before.

The efforts of Morelos and the Mexican Congress to secure aid for the flagging revolution were courageous and determined, but futile from the beginning. The best prospect as a source of aid was the United States because of its traditional sympathy for movements of liberation, but the United States was involved in a war and could offer no help at the time. The Mexican insurgents, therefore, had to rely on adventurers and professional revolutionaries in their bid for assistance from the United States — men who were more often motivated by desire for personal fame and fortune rather than by ideological considerations. As a result, the inexperienced and unsuspecting Mexican insurgents were frequently victimized by members of the New

Orleans clan. No one questions Morelos' objectives or his patriotic efforts in seeking outside aid, but in 1814 and 1815 a greater achievement than he and his associates had effected was necessary to stem the receding revolutionary tide.

REFERENCES

1. See Manuel Puga y Acal, "La fase diplomática de nuestra guerra de independencia," *Revista Mexicana de Derecho Internacional*, I (Sept., 1919), 423-29; and Isidro Fabela, "Los precursores de la diplomacía mexicana," *Archivo Histórico Diplomático Mexicano*, XX (1926), 29-47.
2. Testimony of Morelos, *Morelos documentos*, II, 381.
3. Morelos to Ignacio Ayala, Yanhuitlán, February 17, 1813, Hernández y Dávalos (ed.), *Colección*, IV, 859.
4. Morelos to the captain of the *Aretusa*, Tehuacán, August 27, 1812, *ibid.*, IV, 902.
5. Holmes Coffin to Morelos, December 13, 1812, *ibid.*, p. 903.
6. *Idem* to the governor of Vera Cruz, December 20, 1812, "Documentos sacados del Archivo de Indias sobre la guerra de independencia en Mexico," LAC UT.
7. Testimony of Morelos, *Morelos documentos*, II, 357.
8. Morelos to Ignacio Ayala, Yanhuitlán, February 17, 1813, Hernández y Dávalos (ed.), *Colección*, IV, 859.
9. Simón Tadeo Ortiz to Manuel (*sic*) Morelos, New Orleans, June 18, 1812, *ibid.*, V, 189; *idem* to Joaquín (*sic*) Rayón, June 16, 1812, *ibid.*, pp. 193-94.
10. Luis de Onís to the commander at Nacogdoches, Philadelphia, December 21, 1811, Spanish Archives, No. 119, Archives of the University of Texas.
11. Tadeo Ortiz to Manuel (*sic*) Morelos, New Orleans, June 18, 1812, Hernández y Dávalos (ed.), *Colección*, V, 189-91.
12. There are numerous studies of the revolutionary activities in Texas, 1811-1813, among which may be mentioned: Julia Kathryn Garrett, *Green Flag Over Texas*; Mattie Austin Hatcher, *The Opening of Texas to Foreign Settlement*; and Harris Gaylord Warren, *The Sword Was Their Passport*.
13. Tadeo Ortiz, "Relación general de mi viaje." Archivo General de Indias. Estado — Santa Fé, 57 — Legajo 6 (22). A typescript is in my possession.
14. Manuel (*sic*) Morelos to Tadeo Ortiz, Guaxaca (*sic*), November 29, 1813, Morelos Papers, LAC UT.
15. Pedro Torres Lanzas (ed.), *Independencia de América*, Ser. 1, IV, 58, 76. In the 1820's Tadeo Ortiz published a most illuminating survey of conditions in Mexico in his *México considerado como nación independiente y libre;* and about that time he became extremely active in colonizing projects in Texas. See Edith Louise Kelly and Mattie Austin Hatcher (eds.), "Tadeo Ortiz de Ayala and the Colonization of Texas, 1822-1833," *Southwestern Historical Quarterly*, XXXII (July, 1928), 74-75.
16. Diary of the Guadalupes, November 16, 1813, November 27, 1813, and December 4, 1814, Morelos Papers, LAC UT.
17. "Memoir of Peter Ellis Bean," Yoakum, *History of Texas*, I, 446.
18. *Ibid.*, pp. 447-448.
19. José Antonio Pedroza to Rayón, Nautla, June 21, 1814, Hernández y Dávalos (ed.), *Colección*, V, 547; Morelos to Nicolás Bravo, Agua Dulce, August 26, 1814, José L. Cossío (ed.), "Una carta inédita del Cura Morelos," *Boletín de la Sociedad Mexicana de Geografía y Estadística*, LXII (Sept., 1946), 330.

20. Alamán, *Historia de México*, IV, 100-103.

21. "Memoir of Peter Ellis Bean," Yoakum, *History of Texas*, II, 448-49.

22. Alvarez de Toledo to the revolutionary junta of Mexico, February 10, 1815; *idem* to the President of the United States of Mexico, February 12, 1815; *idem* to Cos, February 15, 1815; *idem* to Rayón, February 15, 1815; *idem* to the junta of rebels of New Spain, February 15, 1815; *idem* to Morelos, March 14, 1815, all in "Papeles dirigidos por el traidor Toledo desde la Nueva Orleans a los cabecillas que componen la junta de rebeldes de Nueva España," typescripts from the Archivo de Indias, in Archives of the University of Texas.

23. "Memoir of Peter Ellis Bean," Yoakum, *History of Texas*, II, 449-50; see also Bennett Lay, *The Lives of Ellis P. Bean*, pp. 98-99.

24. Testimony of José María Morales, *Morelos documentos*, II, 373-74.

25. Testimony of Morelos, *ibid.*, pp. 381-83.

26. The Supreme Mexican Government to President James Madison, Puruarán, July 14, 1815, William R. Manning (ed.), *Diplomatic Correspondence of the United States concerning the Independence of the Latin American Nations*, III, 1596-97.

27. Testimony of Morelos, *Morelos documentos*, II, 382; III, 29.

28. *Ibid.*, II, 382; "Memoir of Peter Ellis Bean," Yoakum, *History of Texas*, II, 450; Warren, *The Sword was their Passport*, pp. 126-28.

29. *Ibid.*, pp. 129-31.

30. Herrera to President Madison, New Orleans, March 1, 1816, Manning (ed.), *Diplomatic Correspondence*, III, 1598.

31. Quoted in Warren, *The Sword was their Passport*, p. 137.

CHAPTER XII

THE LAST DAYS

THE insurgent Congress, having voted to move to Tehuacán to escape the threatening Iturbide and to place itself
in a better position to receive the assistance expected from the
United States, set out from Uruapan on a fateful journey on
September 29, 1815, the day before Morelos' fiftieth birthday.
The entire insurgent government, including a half dozen members of the Congress, three judges of the Supreme Tribunal, and
four secretaries, together with supplies, archives, and currency
was to be escorted by Morelos and his armed forces through
enemy territory by way of Tecpán and the Mixteca. At Huetamo
the convoy was joined by Nicolás Bravo, and the escort was
therefore increased to about a thousand men, half of whom
were armed.[1]

The insurgent party continued on through Cutzamala and
Tlalchapa, and by November 2, it had reached Tenango, about
two-thirds of the distance to Tehuacán. The convoy crossed
the Mescala river, and on the next day arrived at Tesmalaca,
six leagues beyond. Since the group had been on the move
almost continuously for more than a month and had marched
in military formation at the rate of twelve hours a day, and on
scant rations, it voted to take a full day's rest at Tesmalaca.[2]
Joyous over their good fortune thus far, and confident that it
would continue, the party little suspected the impending danger
which was closing in at that very moment.

Meanwhile, Calleja had received word of the insurgent ex-
odus; and although Morelos' clever feints and false moves fooled
him for a while, the viceroy was confident that at least one of
the royalist detachments he had sent out from the capital would
intercept the insurgents in time. His assumption was correct:
Colonel Manuel de la Concha and his force of six hundred men

accidentally picked up the trail of the insurgent convoy, and by forced marches came within sight of Tesmalaca on the morning of November 5, just as the insurgents were leaving.[3]

The sight of the royalist force was so shocking to the insurgents that they would have fled in all directions at once had it not been for Morelos' leadership. He took immediate steps to send the deputies, the baggage, and the noncombatants ahead, while setting up his defenses in preparation for battle. Placing one division on the right and one on the left, he himself remained in the center with a division and the only two cannon the insurgents had. Colonel Concha gave the order to charge; the right wing of the insurgents gave way, broke into flight, and carried part of the center with it. A second charge of the royalists through the insurgent's broken lines caused all remaining resistance to collapse. Seeing that all was lost, Morelos cried out to Bravo, "Go save the Congress; it matters not if I perish." Ordering those about him to flee for their lives, Morelos himself spurred his horse in the direction of a steep hill. At the base he stopped to dismount, but as he was removing his spurs to facilitate the climb on foot, he was halted suddenly by a squad of royalist soldiers under Lieutenant Matías Carranco, who had served Morelos at Acapulco and Cuautla. Resistance at that point was futile. As Morelos made known his willingness to surrender, he eyed his captor and remarked laconically, "Señor Carranco, it appears that we know one another."[4]

Many other prisoners besides Morelos were taken, including José María Morales, the chaplain of the Congress, but the members of the Congress were far enough ahead at the time to escape. Under the escort of Nicolás Bravo, the Congress at length arrived at Tehuacán on November 16,[5] but that mattered little to the royalists, who had captured the main prize. The surrender of Morelos was the greatest loss the insurgents had suffered since the capture of Miguel Hidalgo.[6] The royalist who participated in the action of Tesmalaca were later rewarded liberally with promotions and honors.[7]

Morelos and Morales were taken to Tenango, where they were forced to witness the execution of twenty-seven prisoners who had been taken in the Tesmalaca disaster. Then the captives were shackled on muleback and escorted to Tepecuacuilco, where they were imprisoned for several days while the royalists waited for orders from Calleja. At length Concha's itinerary to the capital with his prisoners received viceregal approval, but he was instructed to complete the last four leagues of the journey, from San Agustín de las Cuevas to Mexico City, at night to prevent "an accident" from occurring.[8]

On November 16 the party left Tepecuacuilco, proceeded by way of Cuernavaca, and arrived at the capital in the early morning hours of November 22. Morelos and Morales were confined immediately to the secret prisons of the Inquisition where they could be closely guarded.

By the time the captive Morelos was led into Mexico City, he had become the subject of a heated three-cornered dispute involving the military power, the ecclesiastical authority, and the Inquisition, each of which stoutly defended its prerogatives, and insisted that the Morelos case fell exclusively within its own jurisdiction. Viceroy Calleja, representing the civil and military authority, desired an expeditious trial in which no time would be lost in convicting Morelos of treason and in sentencing him to death. But Pedro de Fonte, Archbishop-elect of Mexico and head of the ecclesiastical hierarchy, was vitally concerned with the case because of Morelos' sacerdotal status, and insisted that the ecclesiastical authority should take precedence over the civil power. Finally, the Inquisition, only recently restored in Mexico, took a lively interest in the case and viewed it as an unparalleled opportunity to recover prestige for that office. Calleja therefore recommended a compromise whereby Morelos was to be examined and tried first by a joint tribunal representing both the civil and ecclesiastical jurisdiction, and the trial was to be concluded within three days.[9]

The trial began at eleven o'clock on the morning of November

22. For the remainder of the day Morelos, with his characteristic composure, answered the charges of his inquisitors. Accused of having committed the crimes of treason, of disloyalty to the king, and of promoting independence, Morelos replied that since there was no king when he joined the revolution, he worked enthusiastically for the cause of independence, assuming that there was no one against whom he could commit the crime of treason. He continued to support the independence movement, he said, because he did not expect Ferdinand VII to return to Spain. Morelos was certain that even if the king had returned, he would have become a corrupted man and a bad Catholic. Before he decided in favor of independence Morelos said that he consulted some intellectuals, who assured him that the cause was justified, since Ferdinand was guilty of surrendering Spain and himself to Napoleon. Respecting the report of Ferdinand's return to Spain in 1814, Morelos said that at first he had not believed it; after he had verified the story, he had dismissed it on the grounds that the king had returned as a "Napoleónico."

With regard to the charge that Morelos had shot royalist leaders in Oaxaca and Orizaba, and had executed persons in southern Mexico, he answered that he had ordered those executions in compliance with instructions from the Supreme Junta in the case of the first two places, and in agreement with the Congress of Chilpancingo with respect to the last. The slaughter of persons along the southern coast, he maintained, were not executions, but reprisals for the death of Matamoros. He denied that as a member of the executive power he had given orders for the burning of towns and haciendas. He had ignored the edicts of excommunication because he considered them invalid, for it was his impression, he said, that only the Pope or a general council of the Church could impose them on an independent nation. As to the specific edict of Abad y Queipo of July 22, 1814, which declared Morelos a heretic, he explained that he had ignored the edict, since he had never considered Abad a consecrated bishop. The bloodshed, the destruction of fortunes, the separation of families, and the desolation of the country, he said, were unfortunate but inevitable results of any revolution, and in the beginning he did not anticipate so much destruction. Asked if he had celebrated mass during the revolution, Morelos answered that he had done so regularly until the bloodshed began; after that, he had not celebrated mass a single time.[10]

A formal defense was presented for Morelos on the next day, November 23. His attorney was José María Quiles, a youth who was still a law student in the university. Quiles believed that any attempt to deny the charges against Morelos was completely futile; but while he admitted that the defendant had committed many errors, Quiles tried to show that they were largely the result of bad judgment and misinformation. The young lawyer with considerable skill based the greater part of his defense on the decree of Ferdinand VII of May 4, 1814, which invalidated all legislation passed by the Spanish Cortes, an authority which both the king and Morelos, though for different reasons, opposed and refused to recognize. The implication was that Morelos should not be censured too severely for opposing something which the king had considered illegal. Quiles then concluded with a statement which has caused no end of controversy. According to the record, he said that if Morelos' life should be spared, he would disclose military plans that would enable the royalists to pacify the country in a short time.[11] What is the explanation for this statement? Was it an indiscretion on the part of a young, inexperienced lawyer? Did Morelos have anything to do with it? Or was it a royalist fabrication? Morelos, of course, was not particularly concerned about saving his life, but by that time, in anticipation of being degraded from the priesthood, he probably had become concerned about his soul. Perhaps Quiles, knowing that Morelos was willing to make concessions, hoped to save his client's life as part of the bargain, inasmuch as the young lawyer seemed to be more interested in saving Morelos' life than Morelos was.

Morelos' trial before the united jurisdictions was concluded at noon on November 23, and the testimony was submitted to Pedro de Fonte, Archbishop-elect of Mexico, who was to pass a sentence of degradation, in accordance with arrangements already made with the viceroy, and then deliver the prisoner to the civil authority. The archbishop-elect appointed a *consultiva* composed of seven church dignitaries, including himself, which deprived the accused of all offices and benefits, and subjected him to solemn degradation, an act to be performed by his old enemy, Antonio Bergosa y Jordán, the Bishop of Oaxaca. Yet the *consultiva*, apparently apprehensive about shedding priestly blood, recommended to the viceroy that Morelos' life be spared.[12]

At that point the Inquisition, that traditional defender of orthodoxy, entered the picture. Its chief inquisitor, Manuel de Flores, welcomed the Morelos affair as an opportunity to recover some of that tribunal's shattered prestige. "No time was lost," says Henry Charles Lea, "in commencing the most expeditious trial in the annals of the Holy Office — a grim comedy to gratify the vanity of the actors."[13] On November 23, Fiscal José Antonio Tirado, presented the *clamosa*, which charged that Morelos had signed the Constitution of Apatzingán, as well as other heretical publications; that he had celebrated mass while under a ban of excommunication; and that when the Bishop of Puebla had denounced him for doing so, he had replied that it would be easier to get a dispensation after the war than to survive the guillotine; and that he had been declared a heretic by the Bishop-elect of Michoacán.[14]

Later that same morning Morelos was brought before the awesome tribunal of the Inquisition, which consisted of ten distinguished churchmen. He was warned to tell the truth "for the love of God and the Virgin in order to save his soul." By the afternoon of the following day (November 24) he had been subjected to three hearings. Then the accusation consisting of twenty-six charges was presented by Fiscal Tirado. Since Morelos had forsaken the doctrines of the Church in favor of the heresies of Hobbes, Helvetius, Voltaire, Luther, and other pestilential writers, the charges stated, the accused was declared a heretic, apostate of the holy faith, an atheist, materialist, deist, libertine, implacable enemy of Christianity and the state, a vile seducer, hypocrite, and traitor.[15]

For the remainder of that day and half of the next, Morelos attempted to answer the charges. The insurgents had opposed only French domination of Spain, he said, and the restoration of Ferdinand VII was, in his opinion, another aspect of Napoleonic duplicity. The ban of excommunication was based on false charges, he insisted, and consequently was invalid; since the war had interfered with the due observance of bulls and religious ceremonies, he had attempted to provide the people with spiritual care sufficient for their needs. His own life had been irregular, he admitted, but he did not think it was scandalous. Although he had sent his son to a Protestant country for his education, he had instructed him to go to a Catholic school.[16]

From a list of three lawyers assigned to handle Morelos' defense, he chose José María Gutiérrez de Rosas, who was allotted three hours to prepare his case. On that same afternoon (November 25) the attorney denounced the insurrection and the Cortes, expressed the hope that Morelos might be extended absolution in view of his penitent heart, and spent the rest of his time apologizing for the embarrassing position in which he had been placed. The prisoner was then led back to his cell, and the sentries were alerted to guard against any attempt by Morelos to commit suicide by taking poison.[17]

The consulta de fé met the next day to pass sentence. It unanimously agreed that a public auto de fé should be held at eight o'clock the next morning for the act of degradation in the presence of the inquisitors and several hundred distinguished guests selected by Flores. The consulta announced that Morelos was guilty of malicious, pertinacious, and imperfect confession, of heresy, of profaning the sacraments, and of high treason, human and divine. He was ordered to attend mass in the guise of a penitent, and to present a green candle, symbolizing a heretic, to the priest. His property was to be confiscated; and should the viceroy spare his life, he was to be banished from America and imprisoned for life in an African garrison. He was to be deprived of all ecclesiastical benefits; his three children were to be declared infamous, and their descendants were to be subject to legal disabilities. He was to make a general confession, and for the rest of his life he was to recite the seven penitential psalms on Fridays, and a part of the rosary on Saturdays. A tablet, inscribed with his name and crimes, was to be suspended in the cathedral so that all posterity could view his wicked deeds.[18]

From that time on, Morelos, a good Catholic who was deeply concerned about salvation, began to weaken. Examined a second time by the united jurisdictions, immediately after he had heard the sentence of the Inquisition, Morelos began to divulge the military information which Quiles had promised in his defense. He mentioned fifteen insurgent commanders by name and gave details about the size and location of their armies. He said that he considered José Manuel Terán and Ramón Rayón as the two most effective officers, but added that he had much respect for others like Guadalupe Victoria, Pablo Galeana, Remigio Yarza, and Francisco Osorno. Nicolás Bravo, he thought, lacked the qualities of the others, but was a popular and courageous leader. The insurgent forces, declared Morelos, were sustained primarily by the produce of the haciendas which had belonged to captured Europeans. Although booty and contributions had brought in some revenue, import duties and the *alcabala* had produced but little. Asked about insurgent relations with the United States, Morelos admitted that vigorous efforts had been made to get help, but that nothing had been accomplished.[19]

The *auto de fé,* held on the morning of November 27 and witnessed by several hundred of the most distinguished persons in the capital, was an imposing and awesome spectacle.[20] The prisoner entered the room in penitential robes; he knelt during the ceremony of reconciliation while the *miserere* was recited and the gentle strokes of purification were applied. After mass was celebrated, there came the terrible and agonizing act of degradation, performed by Antonio Bergosa y Jordán, who burst into tears. There were unmistakable signs of emotion on Morelos' face for the first time since the beginning of the ordeal. Bishop Bergosa wrote a full report of the proceedings to his king, and humbly requested royal approval for what he had done "so that it would serve as a guide to the bishops of Mexico, in view of the most difficult and disagreeable circumstances which have ever been encountered in this capital."[21]

Morelos then was returned to the secret prisons of the Inquisition under heavy guard and with shackles about his legs. At two o'clock in the morning he was transferred, strongly guarded, to a cell in the artillery barracks, a move which signified that his fate now rested with Viceroy Calleja and the state. The Inquisition had done its work. "It might be said," wrote Father Miguélez, "that the Mexican Inquisition, for a few moments, had been brought back to life to condemn Morelos and then had been returned to the grave to await there the verdict of History. For although it had some merits during its life, it was a pity for its good name that it could not have died with greater dignity."[22]

Morelos' trial by the state began on Monday morning, November 28. The twenty-one questions which Calleja had prepared included subjects such as: why the accused had joined the revolution, his military plans and operations, his formation of the Congress of Chilpancingo, his relations with the Congress, the size of insurgent forces, relations with foreign powers, his attitude toward the restoration of Ferdinand VII, and his recommendations for the pacification of the country.[23]

The testimony of Morelos in answer to the charges continued for three days, and it was recorded by Alejandro de Arana, who served as secretary. The extended account is an unbelievably complete and accurate description of Morelos' military, political,

and diplomatic activities from 1810 to 1815, and thus it consti-
tutes one of the most valuable sources of information about the
movement for independence and Morelos' role in it. While the
testimony contains a number of inaccuracies and inconsistencies,
one cannot fail to be amazed at the memory of the man, who
was able to relate, even under those trying circumstances, an
extraordinary amount of detail, including numbers of men, guns,
prisoners, wounded, killed, and the like, covering a five-year
period. Perhaps most of the interminable number of hours he
sat in his cell were spent in reflecting on his past and in preparing notes which would aid his memory during the next day's
recitation of his activities.[24]

On the morning of December 1, Morelos again divulged vital
military information as he had done before the united jurisdiction on November 26. He added that the province of Valladolid
could be subdued easily with the immediate dispatch of one
division, so desirous were the people there for the restoration
of order and peace. Offered pardons, they would return to the
royalist fold. The royalist troops at Tecpán, he advised, should
advance on Zacatula and should join a division from Tlacotepec
after the country around the Balsas had been subdued. The
royalist force at Huajuapán, he said, should attempt to prevent
Sesma and Guerrero from reconquering Oaxaca; and Terán, who
was in Tehuacán, should be prevented from uniting with Guadalupe Victoria. Morelos concluded by saying that he could give
no advice regarding the coast of Vera Cruz, Llanos de Apán,
Nueva Galicia, or Nuevo Santander, because he was unfamiliar
with the military situation in those places.

Thus, again it may be said that Morelos had weakened. But
in that regard the historian Genáro García may have been close
to the truth when he wrote that the object of Morelos in revealing vital information was not to save his life but to win favor
with God. Those who were named, said García, did not condemn
Morelos for what he had said; if they had been in his place, they
would have done the same thing.[25] For it must be remembered

that Morelos had been born and reared as a good Catholic, educated in the doctrines of the Church, and that he had served as its obedient servant in the capacity of priest for more than twelve years. As a revolutionist, he continued to insist that he had no quarrel with the Church or its doctrines; but now as an accused man, the most awesome ecclesiastical tribunal in Christendom had labeled him a heretic and degraded him from the priesthood. Worldly and finite matters lost their significance and became secondary; his only concern now in these final days was making peace with his God.

After Morelos had been returned to his cell, a group of persons motivated by curiosity persuaded the sentries to let them view the prisoner, but when their language became vile and insulting, the viceroy ordered that no one else was to be allowed entrance. At the insistence of the archbishop, the viceroy granted sufficient time in Morelos' prison routine for the holding of spiritual exercises in his cell.[26]

By this time the request of the state was in Calleja's hands. Dated November 28 and drafted by Auditor Miguel Bataller, it sought the death sentence and confiscation of all property. The proposed order also provided that the head of the prisoner was to be amputated and placed in an iron cage and put on exhibit in the plaza of the capital, and his right hand was to be severed and prepared for similar display in Oaxaca.[27]

For almost three weeks, Calleja delayed. Perhaps he thought he could extract more information from his prisoner; or he might have procrastinated, hoping that the insurgent leaders, unaware of Morelos' small regard for his life, would forsake the revolution and accept a pardon in the belief that the life of the captured first chief might be spared. At any rate, the viceroy certainly had no scruples about prolonging the agony. A retraction of Morelos, supposedly written and signed on December 10 and published after his death, in which he asked for forgiveness and stated that at the time of his capture he was preparing to seek a pardon from Ferdinand VII, seems utterly incredible and is questioned even by Alamán.[28] Apparently on December 12, however, Morelos disclosed additional vital information, such as the location of the principal insurgent mineral deposits, the chief mining operations, furnaces, and ammunition caches.[29]

At length, on December 20, Calleja approved the death sentence, but in consideration of representations from the arch-bishop, the decree provided that execution was to take place outside the capital, and that the body should be buried without dismemberment. On the next day, as Morelos knelt in prayer, he heard the sentence which he had regarded as virtually inevitable from the moment of his capture. A confessor was then called.[30]

At six o'clock on the following morning, December 22, a coach which carried Father Salazar and two officers, including Manuel de la Concha, stopped in front of the prisoner's cell. Still in heavy shackles, Morelos was placed aboard and escorted along the road leading to the village of Guadalupe, the site of the church of the patron saint of the Indians. Morelos began to repeat the prayers and the psalms he knew by heart. The intensity of his recitations increased as each community was approached, since he did not know where the sentence was to be carried out. The coach stopped at Guadalupe, but then continued on to San Cristóbal Ecatépec, a short distance to the north. Morelos suddenly realized that this was the final stop.

The commander of the local garrison was not prepared for his guests, so Morelos was quartered in a room full of hay while preparations for the execution were being completed. There was time for a bowl of soup. Just then, the *cura* of the town appeared, and both he and Morelos began to pray. They were interrupted by the movements of the firing squad now taking their positions just outside the window. Before prayers could be resumed, an armed escort entered the room to lead the prisoner to the place of execution.

After Morelos made a short confession to Father Salazar, the prisoner's cloak was removed; his eyes were covered with a white handkerchief; and his arms were bound behind his body with gun slings. His shackles made walking so difficult that he was carried to an enclosure behind the building which formed a sort of parapet. The next thing Morelos heard was the voice of the commander of the escort, as he made a mark on the ground with his sword: "Put him on his knees here." Morelos asked, "Must I kneel here?" To which Father Salazar replied, "Yes, here." Morelos then knelt, and as he raised his head upward in prayer, he uttered his final words: "Lord, thou knowest if I have done well; if ill, I implore thy infinite mercy." The officer gave the command; four shots rang out; and the kneeling Morelos crumbled forward to the ground. Yet his body still moved, and another volley was necessary to take his life.[31]

The body was covered with Father Salazar's cape and was buried that afternoon in the chapel annex of the village parish church. There his remains lay until a congressional decree of July 23, 1823, ordered that they be removed, together with those of other heroes of the independence movement, to Mexico City and be deposited in urns in the Cathedral of Mexico under the Altar of the Kings. Some years later, Morelos' remains, as well as those of the other heroes, were transferred officially to a crypt at the base of the column dedicated to the leaders of independence on the Paseo de la Reforma. But there is some reason to believe that Morelos' remains were not among those which were moved — that they had already been moved by Juan Almonte to a secret grave which is still unknown.[32]

The name of José María Morelos has been honored with one of the highest places in the history of his country. In 1823 he was declared *benemérito de la patria;* in 1828 the name of his birthplace, Valladolid, was changed to Morelia in his honor; and in 1862 the state of Morelos was created out of a portion of the old state of Mexico. He has been the subject of an extensive patriotic oratory and literature to praise his name and to perpetuate his memory.

If Morelos had lived to the year 1821, [wrote Porfirio Díaz in 1891] Iturbide would not have been able to take control of the national insurrection; and the nation would not have passed through a half century of shameful and bloody revolution which caused it to lose half of its territory. Today it would be the powerful republic which we would have expected from seventy years of development initiated by the courage, the abnegation, prudence, and political skill, of which that extraordinary man was the model.[33]

Former President Lázaro Cárdenas, who was and still is a great admirer of Morelos, authorized the erection of a gigantic statue of the hero on the island of Janítzio in Lake Pátzcuaro. With right arm lifted majestically, it towers over the Michoacán countryside, and honors one of the greatest leaders of the Mexican revolution for independence, and one of Mexico's most outstanding men, José María Morelos — priest, soldier, statesman.

REFERENCES

1. Testimony of Morelos, *Morelos documentos*, II, 354-55.
2. Félix de la Madrid to Calleja, Izúcar, November 24, 1815, Gustavo Salas (ed.), "Documentos de la guerra de independencia," *Boletín del Archivo General de la Nación*, XIII (April, 1942), 250-57.
3. Manuel de la Concha to Calleja, Tepecuacuilco, November 13, 1815, *Morelos documentos*, II, 289-90.
4. Bustamante, *Cuadro histórico*, III, 219-20.
5. Nicolás Bravo to his sister, Tehuacán, November 17, 1815, *Morelos documentos*, II, 300.
6. The Congress made an offer to Calleja that it would stop the bloodshed if he would be lenient and spare Morelos' life; should he refuse, the insurgents threatened to slaughter 70,000 Spaniards. See the Congress to Calleja, Tehuacán, November 17, 1815, in Peñafiel, *Ciudades y capitales*, p. 99-100.
7. Calleja to the Royal Tribunal, Mexico City, November 25, 1815, *Morelos documentos*, II, 299.
8. Calleja to Concha, Mexico City, November 19, 1815, *ibid.*, p. 304.
9. Proceedings of the United Jurisdictions, November 22, 1815, Hernández y Dávalos (ed.), *Colección*, VI, 58-66.
10. *Ibid.*
11. Defense of José María Quiles, November 23, 1815, *ibid.*, pp. 66-68.
12. Sentence of the *consultiva*, November 24, 1815, *ibid.*, p. 47.
13. Henry Charles Lea, "Hidalgo and Morelos," *American Historical Review*, IV (1898-99), 648.
14. Petition of Fiscal Tirado, November 23, 1815, *Morelos documentos*, III, 5-8.
15. Accusation of Fiscal Tirado, November 24, 1815, *ibid.*, pp. 16-27.
16. Testimony of Morelos, November 24 and 25, 1815, *ibid.*, pp. 27-32.
17. Defense of José María Gutiérrez de Rosas, November 25, 1815, *ibid.*, pp. 33-36; see also Manuel Flores to Calleja, November 24, 1815, *ibid.*, II, 311.

18. Sentence of the Inquisition, November 26, 1815, *ibid.*, III, 36-38; H. C. Lea, "Hidalgo and Morelos," pp. 650-51.

19. Testimony of Morelos, November 26, 1815, *ibid.*, II, 378-84.

20. Lea, "Hidalgo and Morelos," pp. 650-51.

21. Bishop Bergosa to Ferdinand VII, December 3, 1815, "Documentos sacados del Archivo de Indias sobre la guerra de independencia," LAC UT.

22. Manuel Miguélez, *La independencia de México*, p. 128.

2ʔ Calleja to Concha, November 27, 1815, *Morelos documentos*, II, 327-30.

24. This testimony was first published by Carlos Bustamante as *Historia militar del General Don José María Morelos*.

25. Genaro García, "Morelos," *Anales del Museo Nacional de Arqueología, Historia, y Etnografía*, Ser. 2, I (1922), 198.

26. Alamán, *Historia de México*, IV, 330.

27. Petition of Auditor Bataller, November 28, 1815, *Morelos documentos*, II, 384-85.

28. Alamán, *Historia de México*, IV, 332. The published retraction may be found in the *Gaceta del Gobierno de Mexico*, XXXII (December 26, 1815), 1298-1402.

29. Testimony of Morelos, December 12, 1815, Morelos Papers, LAC UT.

30. Sentence of Calleja, December 20, 1815, *Morelos documentos*, II, 385-87.

31. Alamán, *Historia de México*, IV, 333-34. In the Latin American Collection of the University of Texas there is a Latin testament which contains the following inscription inside the cover: "This book belonged to the apostate José María Morelos Pavón, who was executed on this day on the outskirts of this town as a traitor to his country and to his king. San Cristóbal Ecatépec. December 22, 1815. Alfonso de Quiros, notary."

32. Teja Zabre, *Vida de Morelos*, p. 298.

33. Inscription of Porfirio Díaz, September 30, 1891, in a testimonial *Album* in honor of Morelos, located in the Casa de Morelos in Morelia.

BIBLIOGRAPHICAL ESSAY

THIS BIOGRAPHICAL STUDY of José María Morelos is based to a large extent on published source materials, two of which stand out above all others. One is the three-volume collection of documents by Luis Castillo Ledón entitled *Morelos documentos inéditos y poco conocidos* (Mexico City: Secretaría de Educación Pública, 1927); the other is the six-volume collection edited by Juan E. Hernández y Dávalos called *Colección de documentos para la historia de la guerra de independencia de México de 1808 á 1821* (Mexico City, 1877-1882). These have been supplemented by printed documentary collections of a more specialized nature, manuscript materials, the writings of Morelos' contemporaries, and secondary works such as the standard multi-volume histories of Mexico in the nineteenth century, monographs, biographies, and periodical literature.

In addition to the collections of Luis Castillo Ledón and Hernández y Dávalos, a valuable single volume has been edited by Martín Luis Guzman entitled *Morelos y la iglesia Católica* (Mexico City, 1948), in which the documents pertaining to the *capellanía* were published for the first time. Genaro García has edited a seven-volume collection called *Documentos históricos Mexicanos* (Mexico City, 1910), which contains facsimiles of insurgent newspapers; and Volume XII of his thirty-six-volume collection called *Documentos para la historia de México* (Mexico City, 1907) includes important correspondence between Morelos and Carlos Bustamante. José M. Coéllar has edited the proceedings of the trial of Matamoros in his *Proceso del Caudillo de la Independencia Don Mariano Matamoros* (Mexico City, 1918), and has published a number of facsimiles of documents relating to Morelos in *Autógrafos de Morelos* (Mexico City, 1918). Enrique Arreguín's *A Morelos — Importantes revelaciones históricos* (Morelia, 1913), a collection of documents relating to Morelos' training for the priesthood, is still useful. Pedro de Alba and Nicolás Rangel published documents on the constitutional developments of the independence period in their *Primer centenario de la Constitución de 1824* (Mexico City, 1924). The publications of the Archivo General de la Nación, the Instituto Nacional de Antropología e Historia, and the Sociedad Mexicana de Geografía y Estadística have brought to light significant materials from time to time.

Most of the Morelos materials in the Archivo General de la Nación were published in either the Castillo Ledón or the Hernández y Dávalos collections, or both, but the greater part of the remaining materials were collected by the Mexican bibliographer Genaro García, whose vast library eventually became the nucleus of the Latin American Collection of the University of Texas. Included in these materials are "The José María Morelos Papers, 1795-1815," and "Documentos sacados del Archivo de Indias sobre la guerra de independencia en México." Twenty-seven of the known thirty-two letters written by the Guadalupes are in the "Morelos Papers." In the Hernández y Dávalos manuscript collection at the University of Texas (Exp. 16-7, No. 3664.733) is the *Relación histórico de lo acontencido al Lic. D. Juan Nepomuceno Rosains como insurgente;* and the Joaquín García Icazbalceta Collection has the "Informe del Exmo. Sr. Virrey D. Felix Calleja sobre el estado de la Nueva España dirigido al Ministerio de Gracia y Justicia en 18 de Agosto de 1814." In the Spanish Archives (No. 119), in the Archives of the University of Texas, is the correspondence of Luis de Onís which deals with Simón Tadeo Ortiz; also typescripts from the Archivo General de Indias of the correspondence of Alvarez de Toledo with the Mexican insurgent leaders. The staff of the Archivo General de Indias in Seville, Spain, very graciously made for the author typescripts of the five Guadalupe letters not included in the Morelos Papers, as well as the correspondence of Simón Tadeo Ortiz, including his "Relación general de mi viaje." The San Jacinto Museum of History, San Jacinto Monument, Texas, possesses miscellaneous letters of Morelos, as well as the documents covering the Guadalupe negotiations with the viceroy in 1812, entitled "Papeles cogidos al rebelde Morelos sobre el estado de opinión y proyectos formados en esta capital en fines del año de 1812." In the Archivo de Arzobispado de Valladolid in Morelia, a magnificent collection of ecclesiastical records and books, which is still largely unorganized and uncatalogued, three important documents have come to light recently, and there may well be others: one is a "Padrón general de la feligresía de Carácuaro, sus pueblos, y ranchos, y sus haciendas, y estancias por este año de 1798" by Eugenio Reyes Arroyo; the second is a request by Morelos for a chaplain for the hacienda of Cutzián, and the third is a request to transfer the capital of the parish of Carácuaro to Nocupétaro.

The most important and most productive of Morelos' contemporaries was Carlos María Bustamante, whose works are highly informative, though strongly partisan and frequently flamboyant. The most comprehensive is his *Cuadro histórico del revolución de la America Mexicana* (5 vols. Mexico City, 1843-1846). His other works are *Campañas del General Félix María Calleja* (Mexico City, 1828), *Elogio histórico del General D. José María Morelos y Pavón* (Mexico City, 1822), and *Historia militar del General D. José María Morelos* (Mexico City, 1825), which was the first published account of Morelos' testimony before the civil authority. Other important writings of contemporaries are: *Memoir of Colonel Ellis P. Bean*, first published as Appendix 2 of Vol. I of H. Yoakum's *History of Texas* (New York, 1856); Alejandro de Humboldt's *Ensayo político sobre el reino de la Nueva España* (Edited by Vito Alessio Robles. 5 vols. Mexico City, 1914); Henry G. Ward's *Mexico in 1827* (2 vols. London, 1828); and Anastasio Zerecero's *Memorias para la historia de las revoluciones en México* (Mexico City, 1869).

Of the standard multi-volume secondary accounts which cover the independence period, the most comprehensive and broadest in scope, though conservative in tone, is Lucas Alamán's *Historia de México desde los primeros movimientos que preparon su independencia en el año 1808 hasta la época presente* (5 vols. Mexico City, 1849-1852). Very important also and generally sympathetic to Morelos and the revolution are: H. H. Bancroft, *History of Mexico* (6 vols. San Francisco, 1883-1887); Emilio del Castillo Negrete, *México en el Siglo XIX o sea su historia desde 1800 hasta la época presente* (26 vols. Mexico City, 1875-1892); José María Luis Mora, *México y sus revoluciones* (4 vols. Paris, 1856); and Vicente Riva Palacio, ed., *México á través de los siglos* (5 vols. Mexico City, 1888-1889. Vol. III, titled *La guerra de independencia* is by Julio Zárate). The multi-volume accounts by Francisco de Paula de Arrangoiz and by Niceto de Zamacois in general follow the approach of Lucas Alamán. The most comprehensive treatment of the Church is Mariano Cuevas' *Historia de la iglesia en México* (5 vols. Mexico City and El Paso, Texas, 1921-1928).

There are a number of excellent and valuable monographs dealing with phases of Morelos' career. One is Rafael Aguirre Colorado, et al., *Campañas de Morelos sobre Acapulco* (Mexico City, 1933), a scholarly work which includes in its appendices the important documents from the Archivo General de la Nación which bear on the Acapulco campaigns. A similar study is Luis Chávez Orozco's *El sitio de Cuautla* (Mexico City, 1832). Julián Bonavit,

Fragmentos de la historia del Colegio Primitivo y Nacional de San Nicolás de Hidalgo (Morelia, 1910) treats of Morelos and Hidalgo at San Nicolás. Antonio Peñafiel, *Ciudades coloniales y capitales de la República Mexicana — Estado de Morelos* (Mexico City, 1909) includes documents not available elsewhere; Albert Francisco Pradeau, *Numismatic History of Mexico* (Los Angeles, 1938) deals with Morelos' currency; Juan de la Torre, *Bosquejo histórico y estadístico de la ciudad de Morelia* (Mexico City, 1883) has insights on Morelos' birthplace; J. M. Miguel y Vergés, *La independencia Mexicana y la prensa insurgente* (Mexico City, 1941) covers the role of the insurgent press; and Harris Gaylord Warren, *The Sword Was Their Passport* (Baton Rouge, 1943) is a scholarly treatment of filibustering activities on the frontier of northern Mexico.

The best biographical work on Morelos in any language has been done by Alfonso Teja Zabre, whose first study appeared in 1934, followed by a second in 1946 and a third in 1959. Since each biography is a revision of the older work, and includes the results of the most recent research which Teja Zabre has completed on his subject, each new study is an improvement on the previous one. The biography by Ruben Hermesdorf, called *Morelos — Hombre fundamental de México* (Mexico City, 1958) and the one by Ezequiel Chávez, called *Morelos* (No. 39 in the series entitled *Figuras y episodios de la historia de México,* Mexico City, 1958), are better than the others, such as the one by Victor Esperón or Francisco Urquizo, which are too eulogistic. Four useful biographical sketches are: James Magner, *Men of Mexico* (Milwaukee, 1942); John A. Caruso, *The Liberators of Mexico* (New York, 1954); Nicolás Rangel, *José María Morelos — Caudillo de la independencia* (Mexico City, 1915); and an article by Genaro García in the *Anales del Museo Nacional de Arqueolgia, Historia, y Etnografía,* Ser. 4, I (March-April, 1922), 193-198. The most thorough and up-to-date account of Miguel Hidalgo since José de la Fuente's *Hidalgo intimo* (Mexico City, 1910) is Luis Castillo Ledón's *Hidalgo: La vida del héroe* (2 vols. Mexico City, 1948-1949). For the other revolutionary figures, one should consult Eduardo L. Gallo, ed., *Hombres ilustres Mexicanos* (4 vols. Mexico City, 1873-1874) and Alejandro Villaseñor y Villaseñor, *Biografías de los héroes y caudillos de la independencia* (Mexico City, 1910). Of the voluminous amount of periodical literature, the following articles are of the greatest significance: Alberto María Carreño, "Los primeros pasos hacia la democracía y la independencia Mexicanas, 1810-1813," *Memorias de la Academía Mexicana de la Historia,* III (January-March, 1944), 41-91; Isidro Fabela, "Los precursores de la diplomacía Mexicana," *Archivo Histórico Diplomático Mexicano,* XX (1926), 1-206; José M. de la Fuente, "Un autógrafo de Hidalgo," *Boletín de la Sociedad de Geografía y Estadística,* III (1908), 419-423; Hugh M. Hamill, Jr., "Early Psychological Warfare in the Hidalgo Revolt," *Hispanic American Historical Review,* XLI (May, 1961), 201-235; Germán Latorre, "La separación del virreinato de Nueva España de la metrópoli," *Revista de Archivos, Bibliotecas, Museos,* XXXI (September-December, 1914), 120-221; Henry Charles Lea, "Hidalgo and Morelos," *American Historical Review,* IV (1898-1899), 636-651; Manuel Puga y Acal, "La fase diplomática de nuestra guerra de independencia," *Revista Mexicana de Derecho Internacional,* I (September, 1919), 410-492; and Karl M. Schmitt, "The Clergy and the Independence of New Spain," *Hispanic American Historical Review,* XXXIV (August, 1954), 289-312. The most illuminating of several articles which Alfonso Teja Zabre has written is "Posteridad y presencia de Morelos," *Memoria de la Academía Nacional de Historia y Geografía,* Bol. 1, Año Tercer, Segunda Epoca (1947), 47-58, the greater part of which he later included in his most recent biography, *Vida de Morelos* (Mexico City, 1959).

INDEX